Montesquieu and Rousseau

FORERUNNERS OF SOCIOLOGY

Montesquieu and Rousseau

Forerunners of Sociology

BY EMILE DURKHEIM

Foreword by Henri Peyre

Durkheim, Montesquieu, and Rousseau, by Georges Davy

Note, by A. Cuvillier

ANN ARBOR PAPERBACKS
THE UNIVERSITY OF MICHIGAN PRESS

First edition as an Ann Arbor Paperback 1965

Published in the United States of America by
The University of Michigan Press and simultaneously
in Toronto, Canada, by Ambassador Books Limited
Translated by Ralph Manheim
Manufactured in the United States of America

Foreword

by Henri Peyre

The centenary of Durkheim's birth in 1958 and that of Bergson's in 1959 were not celebrated in France with the fervor or the official pomp which could have been expected. Those two men, working in opposite directions but deeply respectful of each other, have nevertheless done more to reorient French, and even European thinking, than most philosophers within a hundred years. They themselves provided their successors with the tools with which to amend or to transcend their work. The sociologists who have, especially in English-speaking countries, contributed most to the immense, almost fetishist prestige which their discipline has gained in the last three or four decades, have been wary of emulating Durkheim's generalizing power. They have preferred being objective to being normative, empiricism to hypotheses, the patient exhaustive collection of facts to those flashes of insight which lead to a new interpretation of the facts.

But it is questionable which serves science and social science best: the analysis of a great number of facts or the imaginative framing of a fertile hypothesis from a small group of striking facts. Durkheim's re-creation of French sociology and his imperious formulation of methodological rules for that young science gave a splendid impetus to many other "human sciences" or "sciences of man" as the French call them: not ethnology and anthropology alone shared in that renewal, but linguistics with Meillet, Vendryès, Benveniste, geography with Gourou and Dion, political economy with Simiand, law with Davy and Scelle, Celtic, Chinese and classical archeology with Hubert, Granet, Gernet, art history, the history of literature and history proper with Hourticq, Lanson, Febvre. Mauss, whose pioneering research has stimulated many eminent American anthropologists, was Durkheim's nephew and disciple; Halbwachs, whose achievement was varied and far-reaching, like his colleague the sinologist Maspéro, and more recently Lévi-Strauss, while departing from a strict Durkheimian orthodoxy which the master never wished to impose, owed much to Durkheim's peculiar blend of scientific reasoning and of fervor. In no country perhaps has social research proved more creative than in France in those years 1910-30, thanks to an adventurous spirit of objective curiosity and of moral fervor, and, not least of all, to a talent for writing clearly and elegantly which seems to fill social scientists of other lands with distrust. Durkheim was an austere and forbidding professor tirelessly addicted to his life-work; but there was passion in his logic and intense devotion to a moral and even patriotic ideal behind his self-effacing research. Of him and of many other thinkers and scholars who altered the shape of things or of our views on things could be said what he himself declared of French socialists in his posthumous book: *Le Socialisme* (1928) translated in 1958 as *Socialism and Saint-Simon:* "The research was undertaken to establish the doctrine . . . far from the doctrine resulting from the research. It was passion that inspired all these systems, . . . an élan for more justice."

Like Bergson, Emile Durkheim was a Frenchman of Jewish origin whose family roots have been in central or eastern Europe; yet both proved to be French of the French. Durkheim was born in eastern France in Epinal, in the Vosges region in 1858. His father was a rabbi and wished for his son to follow the same vocation. In the secondary school of his native city, young Durkheim became impressed by Catholicism, but soon went over to agnosticism. He was an exceptional pupil, and his teachers directed him toward the Ecole Normale Supérieure. He successfully passed the exacting competitive examination which selected some fifty young men from the whole of France every year, in 1879. Bergson and Jaurès had preceded him there by one year; the logician Goblot, the experimental psychologist Pierre Janet, the linguist Brunot were among members of Durkheim's class. Soon, Durkheim gained ascendancy in that group of gifted young men often addicted to the mockery of naïve enthusiasm. For he had the fervor of a prophet. He was impatient of the narrowly humanistic and complacently literary character of classical studies which "normaliens" had to go through. Philosophy as then taught struck him as superficial and dangerously aloof from science. His eagerness was at one and the same time for more objective first-hand research so as to rest philosophy on a bedrock of scientific knowledge, and to put such speculation and research to pragmatic use. He felt deeply republican at a time when France still smarted under her 1870-71 defeat and when many found the Third Republic unglamorous and yearned for a return to a bellicose monarch.

In 1882 Durkheim passed the competitive examination for the "Agrégation" in philosophy: psychology was and still is traditionally linked with philosophy in France and sociology only became an autonomous discipline thanks to Durkheim's efforts. "Agrégés" then are sent to teach in one of the provincial lycées: Bergson taught in Clermont-Ferrand where he one day had the illumination of time and duration as radically different concepts, after he had explained to his sixteen-year-old pupils Zeno's famous paradox. Durkheim taught successively in three cities close to Paris and spent a fruitful year (1885-86) acquainting himself with German social research and ethical speculation. He appears not to have met his contemporary Simmel, but he admired Wundt's *Ethics*. He wrote assiduously and by 1893 he had his two theses ready: the shorter one, which until the twentieth century had to be written in Latin, was the keen essay on Montesquieu's contribution to sociology here rendered for the first time into English from the French translation. The larger one was an epoch-making volume, *De la Division du Travail Social*. It was the work of a man of science, trained to collect facts and to observe sharply, but also that of a thinker propounding a doctrine and, like most of what Durkheim wrote, the task of a man concerned with moral values and with the establishment of a social basis for moral duties such as solidarity. "The duties of the individual toward himself are in fact duties toward society," declared the author at the end of his book.

A lectureship of social science had been, in 1887, created for Durkheim at the University of Bordeaux. In the land where sociology had been founded by Montesquieu, cultivated by the Encyclopedists, had received its very name from Auguste Comte and counted already original practitioners like Espinas and Le Play, it still aroused distrust in academic circles. Durkheim's career was for many years an incessant fight against conservatism and prejudices: traditional religious or spiritualistic philosophy and the somewhat effete and literary psychology then taught in France felt their security threatened by the ascending new science. That resistance explains a dogmatic fervor in Durkheim's tone and in that of his disciples, and a tendency to formulate general truths and to codify their method into rules, without which the French public, accustomed to reading Descartes, Taine, Claude Bernard, might not have found the upstart discipline dignified enough.

After another volume on one of the phenomena which has continually fascinated sociologists, suicide, *Du Suicide* (1897), Durkheim was called to the Sorbonne in 1902. He had previously, in 1895, formulated the famous rules of sociological research, in *Les Règles de la méthode sociologique*, contending, not that social facts are but things, but that they have to be observed and studied objectively, our concern being for causes, not for teleological ends. Durkheim was severe on the errors of Auguste Comte, who generalized on philosophy of history without ever observing precise societies; but he owed much to the spirit of positivism, which Comte himself had betrayed. As one of Durkheim's disciples, Simiand, formulated it: "no facts without ideas, no ideas without facts." Many of Durkheim's views on religion in elementary societies, although he himself never did any field work, derived illuminating conclusions, in part verified by subsequent field work, from the few facts then reported on Central Australian tribes: they are embodied in a very influential volume, *Les Formes élémentaires de la vie religieuse* (1912).

Meanwhile, both because the title of his chair required it and because Durkheim was anxious to inspire practical reforms and to change his countrymen through education, he had given lectures at the Sorbonne on educational theories in antiquity and in the Renaissance, the age of the Jesuits and the age of Enlightenment. Those two volumes are probably the ablest which exist on the subject; they were published posthumously, in 1938, from the author's lecture notes as *L'Evolution pédagogique en France*. Unfortunately the most important of all French-speaking philosophers on education, Rousseau, was not treated there and Diderot's extraordinary *Plan d'une Université pour le Gouvernement de Russie* (1775-76) was not considered. Durkheim never attained the popular success which, much to Bergson's distress, Bergsonism enjoyed around 1908-12, when on all sides in France and Western Europe, a convergence of original intellectual and artistic efforts was proposing the renovation of poetry, of painting (Fauvism and Cubism), of music (the Russian Gallets, Stravinsky, Schoenberg), of physics, of psychology, of fiction through which the twentieth-century view of man and of the world was revolutionized. He worked quietly but arduously, exhausting his health on his pioneer's work and running the remarkable journal *L'Année sociologique*. The Dreyfus case then rent France asunder; Durkheim (whose wife was *née* Dreyfus) coolly, modestly worked with the liberal intellectuals, mostly Protestants, agnostics and a few Jews, who exploded the fraud perpetrated by imprudent army officers and eventually won the case. But he never lost his serene faith in the destinies of France, and in the duties of the most objective students of sociology, which are to help solve practical issues and to assist men in knowing themselves better through exploring social realities. Sociology was to him, as indeed was economics, a moral science in the broad sense which the French language attaches to the adjective moral. It did not bind man to any determinism; on the contrary: race and heredity were rejected as explanations of man which remain inadequate. Ethics was, in the first two decades of the century, severed from the narrow dependence on religion which conservatives still proclaimed, fearing that any weakening of the religious bond would throw man back to the state of an ignoble savage. Durkheim linked the moral code to society and envisaged it as both immanent and transcendent, as he did society itself. Social sciences may be able to describe accurately and even to predict. But they cannot abdicate their essential function, which is to help man become better.

World War I came as a crushing blow to Durkheim, as it did to many idealists who had fondly hoped that peace was stably implanted in Europe and that the development of a strong socialist movement in Germany would efficiently curb German militarism. He had planned to compose a treatise on ethics; more and more, he had separated culture from mere social environment and described society as "existing exclusively within the minds of individuals," as he wrote in his great work on the elementary forms of religious life. Morality severed from religion had to grow roots as solid and nourishing as those which it once had possessed. In terms reminiscent of Montesquieu and of Rousseau, Durkheim had pinned his faith on the growth of consciousness in modern Western society, through education. Man could then understand that "to be free is not to do what one pleases; it is to be the master of oneself, to know how to act with reason and to fulfill one's duty," as he declared in one of his courses of lectures on Moral Education.

But the lights suddenly went out over Europe. Intellectuals on the two sides of the front of battle became committed. Durkheim, like Boutroux and Bergson, wrote several pamphlets to explain France abroad (*La Science française*, 1915, in which he reviewed French sociology in ten pregnant pages) and to denounce Pan-Germanism. Many of his students were killed in battle. Exactly half of the class of promising young men who had been admitted in 1913 at the Ecole Normale Supérieure was slaughtered. Durkheim's own son, Pierre, who had also been a normalien and planned to specialize in social studies was killed in 1916 in the Balkans. The grief was more than the father's heart could bear. On November 15, 1917, he died.

Professor Georges Davy, one of Durkheim's successors in the chair of sociology at the Sorbonne, and former Dean of the Faculty of Letters, has, with the pious admiration which he retains for his master (he entered the Ecole Normale Supérieure in 1905, a few years before

Durkheim's own son) and with intellectual independence, outlined a remarkable lecture which appears as an essay in this volume, the singular merits and the limitations of Durkheim's thesis on Montesquieu. It must be borne in mind that the date of that slim volume was 1893, and few are the theses which could bear reprinting and reading more than sixty years after they were sustained; and that Latin dissertations in particular usually aimed at displaying the candidate's humanistic culture and his rhetorical gifts but did not often embody the result of original research or profound reflection. Moreover, in the last decades of the nineteenth century, the prevailing intellectual fashion was, in French academic circles, to consider the century of Descartes and Pascal, of Racine and Bossuet as the toweringly great one in France, as the only one fit to train the youth of the country. Taine, after the experience of the Commune which left a deep imprint upon the minds of former liberals, Renan himself who never relished being likened to Voltaire, then Brunetière, Faguet, Doumic and most of the official critics were more than tepid in their attitude to the relativist, agnostic, socially minded eighteenth century. Montesquieu's unpublished papers in his castle of la Brède in Gascony had not been explored; his attitude to the problem of the English Constitution or to the French feudal system had not yet been described in any detail. Durkheim blazed a new trail in hailing Montesquieu as the founder of political (which is to say, also of social) science. He scented a pessimist in his great predecessor, and the final episode of the *Lettres Persanes*, the Troglodytes, reads indeed like a negation of the great idea or myth of the eighteenth century, the myth of progress. He realized the falsity of the common view of the separation of powers as a dogma formulated by Montesquieu and probably even the nostalgic and reactionary character of some of Montesquieu's views on parliaments (in the sense of bodies of magistrates or "noblesse de robe"). But Montesquieu had established political laws on a scientific basis, blown an invigorating breath of freedom over his century and in every way he had been a forerunner. Oliver Wendell Holmes, in prefacing *The Spirit of Laws* in the country where Hamilton, James, Wilson, and Madison had loudly honored Montesquieu, rightly declared: "He was a precursor of political economy. He was the precursor of Beccaria in criminal law. He was the precursor of Burke when Burke seems a hundred years ahead of his time. . . . His book has probably done as much to remodel the world as any product of that eighteenth century, which burned so many forests and sowed so many seeds."

If Montesquieu was only half distrusted in France in 1880-1900, Rousseau appeared to the French traditionalists, between 1880 and 1920, and to a few of their followers among American humanists, as the arch evildoer. His name was anathema to many in the academic circles. His *Contrat Social* was charged with having brought forth Robespierre, Saint-Just and the Terror. The Citizen of Geneva was indicted as a foreign meddler who had never understood French political traditions and had legislated for an abstract man, preaching now individualistic anarchy, now the authoritarian domination of the state. If today our view of Rousseau is more balanced, if the *Contrat Social* is indeed the most often reprinted and debated of French political writings and deserves the careful attention of original thinkers (Bertrand de Jouvenel is one of the latest of them, in a profound and lengthy preface to a Geneva edition of the famous treatise in 1947), credit goes in part to Durkheim's lectures. They must have been delivered at Bordeaux before 1901 and they first appeared in the *Revue de Métaphysique et de Morale* in 1918.

Durkheim, with more penetration than most commentators then showed (Lanson, Beaulavon and the Dane, Hoeffding, excepted), realized that Rousseau's thought was acutely conscious of the social element. His brushing aside of the facts is indeed a methodological device in order not to be fascinated by what is, not to justify it because it *is*, but to point out to men an ideal to be reached. As C. E. Vaughan, in his monumental edition of Rousseau's political writings, justly remarked, "he was the first great thinker to pass under the spell of Montesquieu." The last books of the *Contrat Social*, the very wise and practical treatises on the constitutions of Poland and of Corsica bear witness to that profound impact of Montesquieu, "the one man of modern times who was capable of calling this great, but useless science into being" (*Emile*, V). That great and useless science is the political and social discipline.

Durkheim shows with lucid impartiality that Rousseau perceived that all that comes to man from society can never be withdrawn from him, or else he is reduced to the level of a being of pure sensation, almost an animal. Only the social state, as Durkheim interprets Rousseau's thought, turns man into an intelligent and human being; a precursor of sociology, at least as much as Montesquieu was, Rousseau considered the social order as of a radically different nature from what concerns purely individual facts. "For him, society is nothing unless it be a one, definite body, distinct from its parts."

Appearances to the contrary notwithstanding, many affinities linked Durkheim's scientific language and cool reasoning with the fervid social thought of Rousseau: that is why he could understand with sympathy and insight Rousseau the reformer, the moralist, who viewed political and social problems with more originality than most specialists, because he was also a philosopher, and one who lived his ideas and allowed their contradictions to grow spontaneously like those branches which became more verdant than the original tree from which they stemmed. The image is M. de Jouvenel's, who rightly adds that minds narrowly dedicated to political or to social thought seldom enlighten us as much as those who, being philosophers, suddenly turn to political and social matters, projecting on social affairs their conception of man's nature and of man's fate: "Our quarrels are never so ardent as when they are tied to metaphysics by some link." Like both Montesquieu and Rousseau, and like Auguste Comte himself, Durkheim renovated social thinking because he felt intensely and thought fervently, systematically, with his heart as well as with his brain. And, like Bergson and Durkheim himself, Rousseau knew the power of clear and vivid writing to reach the "common" but invaluable reader, the men and women who will in their turn act upon the ideas offered to them, and someday perhaps change the world and themselves.

Contents

Montesquieu's Contribution to the Rise of Social Science 1

The Conditions Necessary for the Establishment of Social Science 3

To What Extent Did Montesquieu Define the Field of Social Science? 15

Montesquieu's Classification of Societies 24

To What Extent Did Montesquieu Believe That Social Phenomena Are Subject to Definite Laws? 36

Montesquieu's Method 50

Conclusion 61

Rousseau's *Social Contract* 65

The State of Nature 66

Origin of Societies 76

The Social Contract and the Establishment of the Body Politic 92

On Sovereignty in General 105

Of Law in General 116

On Political Laws in Particular 122

Conclusion 135

Notes 139

Durkheim, Montesquieu, and Rousseau, by Georges Davy 144

Note, by A. Cuvillier 155

Montesquieu's Contribution to the Rise of Social Science[1]

Unmindful of our history, we have fallen into the habit of regarding social science as foreign to our ways and to the French mind. The prestige of recent works on the subject by eminent English and German philosophers has made us forget that this science came into being in our country. Not only was it a Frenchman, Auguste Comte, who laid its actual foundations, distinguished its essential parts and named it sociology—a rather barbarous name to tell the truth—but the very impetus of our present concern with social problems came from our eighteenth-century philosophers. In that brilliant group of writers, Montesquieu occupies a place apart. It was he, who, in *The Spirit of Laws*, laid down the principles of the new science.

To be sure, Montesquieu did not discuss all social phenomena in this work, but only one particular kind, namely *laws*. Nevertheless, his method of interpreting the various forms of law is also valid for other social institutions and can, generally speaking, be applied to them. As laws bear upon all of social life, he necessarily deals with almost all aspects of society. Thus, in order to explain the nature of domestic law, to show how laws harmonize with religion, morality, etc., he is obliged to investigate religion, morality and the family, with the result that he has actually written a treatise dealing with social phenomena as a whole.

By this I do not mean to say that Montesquieu's work contains very many propositions that modern science can accept as well-demonstrated theorems. Almost all the instruments we require for exploring the nature of societies were lacking in Montesquieu's time. Historical science was in its infancy and just beginning to develop; travelers' tales about faraway peoples were few and untrustworthy; statistics, which enables us to classify the various events of life (deaths, marriages, crimes, etc.) according to a definite method, was not yet in use. Furthermore, since society is a large living organism with a characteristic mind comparable to our own, a knowledge of the human mind and its laws helps us to perceive the laws of society more accurately. In the last century such studies were all in their barest beginnings. Still, the discovery of unquestionable truths is by no means the only way of contributing to science. It is equally important to make science aware of its subject matter, its nature and method, and to lay its groundwork. This was precisely what Montesquieu did for our science. He did not always interpret history correctly, and it is easy to prove him wrong. But no one before him had gone so far along the way that led his successors to true social science. No one had perceived so clearly the conditions necessary for the establishment of this discipline.

Let us begin by setting forth these conditions.

The Conditions Necessary for the Establishment of Social Science

[I]

A discipline may be called a science only if it has a definite field to explore. Science is concerned with things, realities. If it does not have definite material to describe and interpret, it exists in a vacuum. Aside from the description and interpretation of reality it can have no real function. Arithmetic is concerned with numbers, geometry with space and figures, the natural sciences with animate and inanimate bodies, and psychology with the human mind. Before social science could begin to exist, it had to be assigned a definite subject matter.

At first sight, this problem presents no difficulty: the subject matter of social science is social "things," that is, laws, customs, religions, etc. However, if we look into history, we find that until quite recent times, no philosopher ever viewed these matters in such a light. They thought that all such phenomena depended upon the human will and hence failed to realize that they are actual things, like all other things in nature, which have their particular characteristics and consequently call for sciences that can describe and explain them. It seemed to them sufficient to ascertain what the human will should strive for and what it should avoid in constituted societies. Accordingly they sought to know, not the nature and origin of social phenomena, not what they actually are, but what they ought to be; their aim was not to offer us as true an image of nature as possible, but to confront our imagination with the idea of a perfect society, a model to be imitated. Even Aristotle, who devoted far more attention than Plato to experience, aimed at discovering, not the laws of social existence, but the best form of society. He starts by assuming that a society's sole object should be to make its members happy through the practice of virtue, and that virtue lies in contemplation. He does not establish this principle as a law which societies actually observe, but as one which they should act upon in order that human beings may fulfill their specific nature. Later, to be sure, he turns to historical facts, but with little purpose other than to pass judgment upon them and to show how his own principles could be adapted to various situations. The political thinkers who came after him followed his example more or less. Whether they completely disregard reality or pay a certain amount of attention to it, they all have a single purpose: to correct or transform it completely, rather than to know it. They take virtually no interest in the past and the present, but look to the future. And a discipline that looks to the future lacks a determinate subject matter and should therefore be called not a science but an art.

I grant that such an art has always involved a certain science. No one has ever maintained that one type of state is preferable to another without attempting to support his preference with proofs, and such proofs are bound to be based on some reality. If, for example, we think democracy superior to aristocracy, we show that it is more consonant with human nature or we point to historical examples demonstrating that nations which enjoyed freedom excelled those which did not, etc. . . . When we proceed methodically—whether to explore nature or to lay down rules of conduct—we revert to things, that is, to science.

But since writers are wont to derive their opinions about these matters from human existence rather than from the state of societies, such science—if one may call it science—usually contains nothing that is truly social. When an author demonstrates that men are born for freedom or, on the contrary, that what they need above all is security, and from this concludes that the state should be constituted in such and such a way, where, in all this, is the social science? Whatever partakes of science in such arguments bears on psychology, and what relates to society is in the nature of art. When any description or interpretation of social phenomena does occur, it plays a secondary role. This applies to Aristotle's theory of the causes underlying the modification or overthrow of political regimes.

Furthermore, when science becomes involved with art, its specific nature is bound to be vitiated; it degenerates into something equivocal. Art is action; it is impelled by urgency, and whatever science it may contain is swept along in its headlong rush. True science does not admit of such haste. The fact is that whenever we have to decide what to do—and such decisions are the concern of art—we cannot temporize for long; we must make up our minds as quickly as possible because life goes on. If the state is sick, it is impossible to keep doubting and hesitating until social science has described the nature of the sickness and discovered its causes; action must be taken without delay. However, we are endowed with intelligence and the faculty of deliberation; we do not make our decisions at random. We must understand, or rather think we understand, the reasons for our plans. Hence we hastily collect, compare, and interpret the facts that come to hand; in short, we improvise a science as we go along, so that our opinion seems to have a foundation. This is the kind of science—greatly adulterated as one can see at a glance—that we find within art. But since we have operated without method, such science offers nothing more than doubtful probabilities, which have such authority as we are willing to accord them. If we act upon them, we do so not because the arguments on which they seem to be based leave no room for uncertainty, but because they fall in with our personal feelings; they invariably lead in the same direction as our spontaneous inclinations. Moreover, when our personal interests are at stake, everything stirs our emotions. When something seriously affects our personal existence, we are unable to examine it carefully and calmly. There are things we like, others we detest, still others we desire, and to every situation we bring our likes, dislikes and desires, all of which are obstacles to reflection. Furthermore, there is no hard and fast rule that might enable us to perceive what is most often intrinsically useful and what is not, for one and the same thing is useful in one respect and harmful in another. Since utility and harmfulness cannot be compared mathematically, each individual acts in accordance with his own nature and, following his personal bent, focuses his attention on one aspect of the thing and overlooks the other. Some men, for example, are so fired by the idea of harmony among citizens that they find nothing so important as a strongly unified state and are not troubled by the suppression of freedom it may entail. For others, freedom comes first. The collection of arguments by which these men support their opinions do not reflect phenomena, realities, or the actual order of things, but merely states of mind. Such procedure is the opposite of true science.

Science is so different from art that it can be true to its own nature only by asserting complete independence, that is, by applying itself, in utter disregard of utility, to a definite object with a view to knowing it. Far from public or private debate, free from any vital necessity, a scientist must pursue his endeavors in the peace and quiet of his study, where nothing impels him to press his conclusions beyond what is justified by his evidence. Even in abstract questions, no doubt, our ideas spring from the heart, for the heart is the source of our entire life. But if our feelings are not to run away with us, they must be governed by reason. Reason must be set above the accidents and contingencies of life, for otherwise, having less force than the desires of all kinds that animate us, it will inevitably take the direction they impose.

This does not mean that science is useless in the conduct of human life. Quite the contrary. The sharper the distinction between science and art, the more useful science can be to art. What is more desirable for a human being than to be sound in mind and body? Only science can tell us what constitutes good mental and physical health. Social science, which classifies the various human societies, cannot fail to describe the normal form of social life in each type of society, for the simple reason that it describes the type itself; whatever pertains to the type is normal, and whatever is normal is healthy. Moreover, since another branch of science deals with sicknesses and their causes, we are informed not only about what is desirable, but also about what should be shunned and how dangers are to be avoided. Hence, it is important for art itself that science should be separate and, as it were, emancipated from it.

Furthermore, each science must have its own specific object; for if it shared its object with the other sciences, it would be indistinguishable from them.

[II]

Not every subject admits of scientific study.

The first task of science is to describe as they are the realities with which it deals. But if these realities differ among themselves to such a degree that they do not constitute a type, they cannot be described by any rational method. They will have to be considered one by one, each independently of the others. But each individual case involves an infinite number of properties, among which no choice can be made; what is infinite cannot be described. The best we could do would be to treat such realities in the manner of poets and storytellers who depict things as they appear to be, without method or rational procedure. If, on the other hand, the realities can be reduced to a type, they present something which can be accurately defined and which characterizes the type in question, for the features common to all individuals of the same type are finite in number and their essence is manifest. We need only put these individuals together and note their points of agreement. In short, science cannot describe individuals, but only types. If human societies cannot be classified, they must remain inaccessible to scientific description.

It is true that Aristotle distinguished long ago between monarchy, aristocracy and *πολιτέια*. But the kinds of society should not be confused with the different types of state; two cities may be different in kind, though governed in the same way. Thus, certain of the *πόλεις*, the Greek city states, and most of the barbaric nations could rightly be called monarchies and were indeed so called by Aristotle because both groups were ruled by kings. However, they differed in nature. Moreover, a change in a nation's system of government does not necessarily involve a change in the prevailing type of society. Consequently Aristotle's classification of societies tells us nothing about their nature. The later philosophers who dealt with the matter accepted his classification and made no attempt to devise another, because they thought it impossible to compare human societies in any respect other than the form of state. The other factors, morality, religion, economic life, the family, etc. . . . seemed so fortuitous and variable that no one thought of reducing them to types. Yet these factors have a strong bearing upon the nature of societies; they are the actual stuff of life and consequently the subject matter of social science.

[III]

Description, however, is merely the first step in scientific procedure, which is completed by interpretation.

And interpretation requires a further condition which was long thought to be lacking in social phenomena.

To interpret things is simply to arrange our ideas about them in a determinate order, which must be the same as that of the things themselves. This presupposes that an order is present in the things themselves, that they form continuous series, the elements of which are so related that a given effect is always produced by the same cause and never by any other. If we assume, however, that there is no such causal relationship and that effects can be produced without a cause or by any cause whatsoever, everything becomes arbitrary and fortuitous. But the arbitrary does not admit of interpretation. Hence, a choice must be made: either social phenomena are incompatible with science or they are governed by the same laws as the rest of the universe.

This is not the place for a thorough examination of the question. We wish merely to show that if societies are not subject to laws, no social science is possible. And without science, there can be no art unless, in establishing the rules of human life, we call upon some faculty other than our reason. However, since the principle that all the phenomena of the universe are closely interrelated has been tested in the other domains of nature and has never proved to be false, it is also valid, in all likelihood, for human societies, which are part of nature. It seems contrary to any sound method to suppose that there are all sorts of exceptions to this rule, when not a single example is known to us. It has often been argued, to be sure, that necessity is irreconcilable with human freedom, but, as we have shown elsewhere,[2] this argument must be ruled out, for if free will really eliminates law, it follows, since the human will is inevitably manifested in external things, that not only the mind but also the body and inanimate things as well will have to be regarded as alien to all order and hence to science. But today no one would dare to question the possibility of natural science. There is no reason why social science should not enjoy the same status.

Yet men, and even philosophers, are naturally inclined to exclude the principle we have been discussing from social phenomena. We usually think that the only motives underlying our acts are the conscious ones, and we deny the existence of others because we are unaware of them. We take the same attitude toward social institutions, attributing primary importance to the most apparent causes, although these derive their power from other causes. It is a natural tendency to regard what is first in the order of knowledge as first in the order of reality. And in the case of political, legal, and religious institutions, is there anything more manifest, more striking, than the personality of those who have governed states, drafted laws, and established religious ceremonies? Thus, the personal will of kings, lawgivers, and prophets seems to be the source from which all social life springs. Their acts are performed in the sight of all; there is nothing obscure about them. Other social phenomena, however, are much more difficult to perceive. This is the origin of the widespread superstition that a lawgiver endowed with almost limitless power is able to devise, modify, and discard laws as he pleases. Although modern historians have demonstrated that law derives from custom, that is, from life itself, by a process of almost imperceptible development unrelated to the concerted intentions of legislators, this opinion is so deeply rooted in the human mind that many still persist in it. But to accept it is to deny the existence of any determinate order in human societies, for if it were true, laws, customs, and institutions would depend not on the constant nature of the state, but on the accident that brought forth one lawgiver rather than another. If the same citizens under a different ruler could produce a different state, it would mean that the same cause, operating under the same circumstances, had the power to produce different effects; there would be no rational tie between social phenomena.

Nothing has so retarded social science as this point of view, which the philosophers, whether consciously or unconsciously, have also accepted. The other obstacles to which we have referred or which we shall discuss below could not be removed so long as this one remained in force. So long as everything in human societies seemed so utterly fortuitous, no one could have thought of classifying them. There can be no types of things unless there are causes which, though operating in different places and at different times, always and everywhere produce the same effects. And where is the object of social science if the lawgiver can organize and direct social life as he pleases? The subject matter of science can consist only of things that have a stable nature of their own and are able to resist the human will. Where things are infinitely pliable, nothing impels us to observe them and they offer nothing that lends itself to observation. For if they had a character of their own, it would be impossible to manipulate them at will. This explains why for a long time social science was only an art.

But, one may argue, nobody has ever denied that the

science of human nature is indispensable to anyone wishing to govern human beings. Granted. But, as we have shown, such a science should be called psychology and not social science. If social science is really to exist, societies must be assumed to have a certain nature which results from the nature and arrangement of the elements composing them, and which is the source of social phenomena. Once the existence of such elements is granted, our lawgiver vanishes and his legend with him.

[IV]

It is not enough, however, to have a subject matter that is scientifically knowable. If types and laws remain so hidden in the depths of things that there is no way of perceiving them, the science of social phenomena will remain forever in a state of mere possibility. Before it can come into actual being, we must possess a method appropriate to the nature of the things studied and to the requirements of science.

It should not be supposed that such a method comes spontaneously to mind the moment we embark on a science. On the contrary, we find it only after much groping. It was only very recently that the biologists found out how to study the laws of life by observing actual living creatures. Psychology also fumbled a long time before managing to work out a method of its own. Social science faces still greater difficulties. The phenomena it deals with are so diverse that what they have in common seems to be hidden from view. They are so fluid that they seem to elude the observer. Causes and effects are so interwoven that the utmost care must be taken to disentangle them. Moreover, it is impossible to experiment with human societies, and it is not easy to find a method that can take the place of experiment. It becomes clear that the method cannot be established before the science begins to take form; the method issues from the science, though it is also indispensable to the science.

Now let us see to what extent Montesquieu, in *The Spirit of Laws*, met these conditions which are indispensable to science.

To What Extent Did Montesquieu Define the Field of Social Science?

[I]

It seems strange that there should have been so much discussion of Montesquieu's purpose in writing his book, for he states his aim in several passages: "This book deals with the laws, customs and divers practices of all the peoples of the earth. Its subject is vast, for it embraces all the institutions that prevail among human beings." Montesquieu tries to get to the bottom of social phenomena to "seek out their origins and discover their physical and moral causes." As for playing the role of legislator, that, he says modestly, is beyond his powers. Indeed, he is particularly careful not to imitate those who undertake to rebuild society from the ground up: "I write not to censure anything established in any country whatsoever. Every nation will here find the reasons on which its maxims are founded . . . Could I but succeed so as to afford new reasons to every man to love his prince, his country, his laws; new reasons to render him more sensible in every nation and government of the blessings he enjoys, I should think myself the happiest of mortals."

This purpose he achieved so well that he has often been reproached with not finding fault with anything, with having respected reality to such an extent that he never ventured to judge it. Yet he was far from viewing human affairs so serenely, and those who accuse him of such indifference have assuredly failed to grasp the meaning of his work. However, he believed that many customs which differ from ours and which all European peoples now reject have a legitimate basis in the nature of certain societies. He held, for example, that polygamy, false religions, a moderate, humane form of slavery, and many other institutions of this kind have been appropriate to certain countries and periods. He even considers despotism, the form of political regime he most detests, to be necessary for oriental peoples.

From this we should not conclude that Montesquieu held aloof from practical problems. On the contrary, he himself declares that he is trying to determine "the institutions that are most appropriate to society and to each society, . . . those having some degree of virtue in themselves and those having none: and of two pernicious practices which one is more so and which less." This explains why his book deals not only with laws, but also with the rules of human life, not only with science, but with art as well. Indeed, he may with some justification be accused of failing to distinguish sharply enough between art and science. He does not devote one part of his book to what *is* and another to what *ought* to be; art and science are so intermingled that more often than not we pass quite unawares from one to the other. Actually two sets of problems are involved and his habit of discussing them simultaneously has its drawbacks, for they require different methods.

However, this is not the same confusion as prevailed among earlier philosophers. In the first place, Montesquieu's science is really social science. It deals with social phenomena and not with the mind of the individual. This new science is not sufficiently distinguished from art, but at least it exists. And far from being stifled beneath problems involving action, it is the main subject of his book. It is the master and in no way the servant of art, and is thus better able to remain faithful to its specific nature. The author's chief aim is to know and explain what exists or has existed. Most of the rules he sets forth are truths—stated in another language—which science had already proved by its own methods. He is concerned, not with instituting a new political order, but with defining political norms. And what is the function of science if not the definition of norms? Since the supreme law of every society is the welfare of its members, and since a society cannot preserve itself without safeguarding its specific nature, it suffices to describe that nature in order to determine what the society in question should strive for and what it should avoid, for health is always desirable and sickness to be avoided. For example: after having demonstrated that democracy is possible only in small states, Montesquieu had no difficulty in prescribing that a democracy should refrain from overextending its frontiers. As we shall see more clearly later on,[3] it is only in exceptional cases that art replaces science without ample justification.

Moreover, since these rules are established by new methods, they differ greatly from those of earlier writers on politics, who formulated types supposedly transcending all considerations of place or time and suitable to all mankind. They were convinced that one form of political regime, one moral and legal discipline was consonant with the nature of all men, and that all the other forms encountered in history were evil or at best imperfect, and owed their existence only to the inexperience of their founders. This need not surprise us. These writers disregarded history and failed to realize that men are not always and everywhere the same, that on the contrary they are dynamic and diversified, so that differences of customs, laws and institutions are inherent in the nature of things. Montesquieu, however, understood that the rules of life vary with the conditions of existence. In the course of his investigations he observed different kinds of society, all equally "normal," and it never entered his head to lay down rules valid for all peoples. He adapted his rules to each different type of society. Monarchy's food is democracy's poison. Yet neither monarchy nor democracy is in itself superior to all other political regimes. The desirability of one or another form of government depends on particular conditions of time and place.[4]

As we see, Montesquieu was not wholly indifferent to the advantages of the things he described. But he approached these problems with a new method. He did not approve of everything that has ever been done, but decided what was good and what was not on the basis of norms derived from the phenomena themselves and thus corresponding to their diversity.

[II]

Montesquieu draws a sharp distinction between social phenomena and the phenomena studied by other sciences.

To be sure, he sets forth laws which follow from the

nature of man, regardless of the particular form of society in which he lives, and thus pertain to the realm of pure psychology. He calls them laws of nature. They are: the right to preserve one's life or to live in peace, the right to eat, the right to yield to the attraction of the opposite sex, and the right to maintain social relations with one's neighbors. He adds that a certain idea of God is the first of the natural laws in importance if not in chronological order, though its relation to the other laws is not made clear. In any case these factors have their beginning and end in the life of individuals and not in that of society; at most, they prepare the way for social life, for though the instinct that impels us to enter into relations with our fellow men may open the way to society, it does not produce the forms, nature, or laws of society. Social institutions can in no way be explained by such factors. Montesquieu's treatment of this entire problem is hasty and superficial. The matter has no direct bearing on the subject of his work. He touches upon it only in order to define his subject more precisely, that is, to mark it off from related problems.

From the natural laws he sharply distinguishes the laws relating to society, to which he gives a special name because they cannot be inferred from the nature of man. These are the subject of his book, the true object of his inquiry: they comprise the law of nations, civil law, political law, and all the major social institutions. But we must be careful in interpreting Montesquieu's terminology. It is true that he does not apply the term *natural* to these various forms of law, but this does not mean that he regards them as foreign to nature. To his mind they are based on reality, but not in the same way as the natural laws, since they result from the nature not of man, but of societies. Their causes are to be sought in social conditions rather than in the human mind. If, for example, we wish to understand the civil law of a given nation, we must consider the size of its population and the nature of the social ties between its citizens; if our aim is to interpret its political law, we must examine the respective situations of the rulers and of the common citizens, etc. Of course, since societies are composed of individual men, their nature must depend in part on the nature of men. But man himself differs from one society to another; his mentality is not everywhere the same, nor does he have the same desires in monarchy as in democracy or despotism. If Montesquieu applied the word "natural" only to the laws of individual life—as though the other laws did not deserve to be so called—this must be ascribed to the habits of his age. For the philosophers of the time a "state of nature" was the state of man living without society, and "natural laws" were those to which man conformed in such a state. Montesquieu accepted this current use of the term despite the ambiguity it involved.

Montesquieu's view of social phenomena gave rise to a new philosophy of law. Until that time, there had been two schools of thought. According to one, law in general was not rooted in the nature of things but established by the deliberate will of human beings through some sort of original agreement. The other held that only one part of the law was natural, namely the part that could be derived from the general notion of man. Only the nature of individual man seemed sufficiently stable and well defined to serve as a solid foundation for law. Accordingly, this school held much the same opinion as the earlier philosophers. Since only the basic principles—of which there were very few—could be traced to the nature of man, the countless particular laws in which the codes of the various nations abounded, were an artificial human product. These thinkers disagreed no doubt with Hobbes, who denied that man was impelled to social life by a natural drive. Still, they believed that political forms and most social institutions, if not society itself, were products of pure convention. Montesquieu, on the other hand, declares not only the general laws, but also the whole system of laws, past and present, to be "natural." However, he derives the laws from the "nature" not of man but of the social organism. He understood with a wonderful lucidity that the nature of societies is no less stable and consistent than that of man and that it is no easier to modify the type of a society than the species of an animal. Thus it is quite unjust to compare Montesquieu with Machiavelli, who regarded laws as mere instruments that princes can use as they see fit. Montesquieu established law on as firm a basis as Grotius and his disciples, though, as we have said, in an entirely new way.

It is true that in several passages he seems to speak of certain principles, even principles of civil and political law, as if they were self-sufficient and independent of the nature of societies. "Before laws were made," he writes, "there were relations of possible justice. To say that there is nothing just or unjust but what is commanded or forbidden by positive laws is the same as saying that before the describing of a circle all the radii were not equal."

Yet this passage in no way conflicts with the interpretation set forth above. To say that the legal systems of societies are rooted in nature is not to imply that there is no similarity between the laws and customs of different peoples. Just as all societies, even those that are most dissimilar, have something in common, so certain laws are to be found in all societies. These are the laws that Montesquieu considers suitable to society in general. Present wherever society exists, they are implied in the very notion of society and can be explained by it. Hence, their truth can be demonstrated regardless of whether they were actually established by man or whether societies exist or have never existed. It suffices to conceive of them as possible. In another passage, Montesquieu calls these laws *law* in an absolute and universal sense, and declares that they are none other than human reason considered as the power governing all societies. They can be deduced, by sheer force of reason, from the definition of society once we have such a definition. Perhaps it is because they are to be found in all nations and are conceived in a sense as anterior to the establishment of societies that he does not clearly distinguish them from the laws of nature.

There is only one justified objection to this doctrine, namely that it divides law and ethics, which are one, into two parts differing both in origin and in nature. It is not easy to see how they join, particularly since they are often in disagreement. Natural law and civil or political law sometimes demand conflicting attitudes. If they have no common basis, how are we to decide which to obey? Montesquieu seems to think we should give priority to the laws of nature.[5] But why should the nature of man be more sacred in every case than that of society? He leaves the question unanswered. This difficulty did not exist for earlier philosophers, since they derived law from a single principle. But if there are two principles, our life is drawn in two directions, often diametrically opposed. There is only one way out of this impasse, namely to assume that all rules of law and custom, even those pertaining to individual life, result from social existence. But in this point and several others, Montesquieu, despite the novelty of his point of view, remains a captive to earlier conceptions.

Montesquieu's Classification of Societies

[I]

Montesquieu did not classify societies, but rather the ways in which they are governed. Consequently he simply took over the traditional categories with slight modifications. He distinguished three types: the republic—which includes aristocracy and democracy—monarchy, and despotism. Comte criticized him sharply for discarding the plan set forth at the beginning of the book and reverting to an Aristotelian conception,[6] but if we examine the work more closely, we shall see that the resemblance to Aristotle is only apparent.

For one thing, his classification is not, like Aristotle's, based on the number of rulers. Montesquieu regards democracy and aristocracy as varieties of one and the same type, though in the former all the citizens participate in government and in the latter only a small number. But though power is in the hands of a single person in both monarchy and despotism, these forms are not only dissimilar but even antagonistic. Many critics have called this distinction confused and ambiguous, and the charge would be justified if it were true that Montesquieu considered only the political regimes of societies. But his range of vision is far wider, for as he describes them the three types of society differ not only in the number of their rulers and in the administration of public affairs, but in their entire nature.

This becomes apparent as soon as we see how he distinguishes them from each other. Aristotle and his followers derive their classification from an abstract notion of the state, but Montesquieu's is based on phenomena themselves. He derives his three types not from any a priori principle, but from a comparison of the societies known to him from his study of history, from travelers' accounts, or from his own travels. And indeed the meaning he attaches to the terms escapes us unless we first find out what nations he is referring to.

He gives the name "republic" not to all societies administered by all or a part of their members, but to the Greek and Italic city-states of antiquity and the great Italian cities of the Middle Ages. However, he is chiefly concerned with the ancient city-states, and whenever he refers to the republican form, it is clear that he has in mind Rome, Athens, and Sparta. This explains why he assigns both democracy and aristocracy to the category of republics. Since both these forms were to be found in the ancient city-states and in some instances one even succeeded the other in the same nation, it was not possible to separate them completely. Actually the barbaric nations, though frequently governed by the entire body of citizens, are not as we shall see included in the said category, and we may be sure that if Montesquieu had been familiar with the political form of present-day France he would not have regarded it as republican.

As for monarchy, he finds this social structure only among the large nations of modern Europe. He demonstrates that it could not have been known to the peoples of antiquity and that it made its first appearance when the Germans invaded and partitioned the Roman empire. He knew, of course, that the Greeks and Latins had long been ruled by kings, but the nature of their regime struck him as something very different from true monarchy. As for despotism, although in a sense it can grow out of any political form through corruption, he believes that it had a natural existence only in the Orient. He has in mind the Turks, the Persians, and several other Asiatic peoples, to which should be added the nations of northern Europe. But can anyone doubt that the ancient city-states, the oriental kingdoms, and the modern European nations represent three totally distinct types of society?

[II]

Montesquieu distinguishes the three types of society not only because they are governed differently but also because they differ in the number, arrangement, and cohesion of their component parts.[7]

The republican form flourished in small cities and never succeeded in spreading beyond their narrow limits; the ancient cities are examples of this form. The despotic state, on the other hand, is found in large societies that spread over vast areas—the Asiatic nations for example. The monarchic state is of medium size, and though it has a larger population than the republic, it has fewer subjects than the despotic.

Moreover, the structures of these various societies are not the same, nor are their members united by the same ties. In a republic, particularly in a democracy, the citizens are all equal and even alike. The city-state appears to be a kind of block made up of homogeneous components, none superior to the others.[8] All are equally zealous for the common weal. Those who occupy positions of authority are not above the others, for they hold office only for a given time. Even in private life there is little difference between them. Indeed, it is the principle of the republic, or at least the aim for which it strives, that no man's personal resources should too far exceed those of his fellow citizens; for though it is difficult to attain absolute equality, the laws of every republic form a barrier to excessive differences in fortune, and such equality would be impossible without restrictions on individual wealth. The means of all men must be modest if they are to be more or less equal. "Since every individual ought here to enjoy the same happiness and the same advantages," says Montesquieu, "they should consequently taste the same pleasures and form the same hopes, which cannot be expected but from a general frugality."

In such a state, private fortunes play no important role in the lives and thinking of individuals, who are preoccupied rather with the common welfare. Hence, the chief source of the difference among men is eliminated. Even private life is much the same for all; the modest status of all citizens, which is established by law, eliminates almost all stimulus to commerce, which can hardly exist without a certain inequality. Thus the activity of all persons is approximately the same. They till a piece of land, which is of the same size for all, and from this they derive their subsistence. In short, there is no division of labor among the members of the body politic, unless we apply the term to the rotation of public office.

All this is eminently a picture of democracy. As for aristocracy, Montesquieu regards it as a debased form of democracy (the more it resembles a democracy, the more perfect it is), and we can therefore leave it out of account.

It is easy to imagine what the unanimous will of the citizens can accomplish in such a society. The idea of the nation is uppermost in men's minds. Since there is practically no private property, the individual is indifferent to personal profit. There are no antagonistic parties to create disunity among citizens. This is the *virtue* that Montesquieu regards as the basis of the republic. He is referring not to ethical virtue but to the political virtue that resides in love of country and leads men to place the interests of the state above their own. The term lends itself to criticism, for it is ambiguous, but Montesquieu's use of it should not surprise us. Do we ourselves not apply it to any moral attitude that sets limits to excessive self-interest?

In a republic, at all events, all citizens necessarily share this attitude, since everyone is "socially minded"—if we may use the term—and in view of the general frugality self-love has nothing to feed on. That part of the individual consciousness which is an expression of society and which is the same in all persons is broad and powerful. The part which relates to the individual and his personal affairs is weak and limited. The citizens do not have to be spurred on by an external force, but by a natural impulse subordinate their own interests to those of the state.

The nature of monarchy is quite different. Here, all

the functions of private as well as public life are divided among the various classes of citizens. Some engage in farming, others in trade, still others in the various arts and crafts. Some make the laws, others execute them either as judges or governors, and no one is permitted to deviate from his role or infringe upon that of others. Thus monarchy cannot be defined by the power of a single person. Montesquieu adds that even if a society is ruled by one individual, it should not be called a monarchy unless it has fixed laws according to which the king governs and which he may not modify arbitrarily. This implies that there are established orders which limit his power. Though he is superior to them, they must have a power of their own and must not be so far below the ruler as to be unable to resist him. For if there were no barrier to the prince's authority, there could be no law limiting his will, since the laws themselves would be entirely dependent on it. It is this principle that distinguishes monarchy from other political regimes. *Division of labor*, which does not exist in the republic, tends toward its maximum development in the monarchy. Monarchical society may be compared to a living organism, each of whose parts performs a specific function in accordance with its nature.

This explains why Montesquieu considers political freedom to be peculiar to monarchy. The classes—or, to use a contemporary term, the *organs*—of the social body limit not only the authority of the prince, but each other as well. Since each is prevented by the others from growing too powerful and absorbing all the powers of the organism, it is free to develop its special nature, but in moderation. We are now in a position to understand the role played by the famous theory of the division of powers in Montesquieu's thinking. It is merely a particular form of the principle that the various public functions should be performed by different persons. If Montesquieu attaches so much importance to the distribution of authority, it is not in order to eliminate all disagreement between the various powers, but rather in order to foster such rivalry that none among them will be able to rise above the others and reduce them to insignificance.

The social tie in a monarchy cannot be the same as in a republic. Since each class is concerned with a limited area of social life, it sees nothing beyond the function it performs. Men's minds are imbued with the idea of their class rather than that of their country. Each order has only one objective, which is not the common weal but self-aggrandizement. Even the private individual is chiefly concerned with his own interests. While under the republic, the equality of all citizens inevitably results in a general frugality, the diversity of status characteristic of monarchy arouses ambition. Where there are varying degrees of rank, honor, and wealth, each individual has before his eyes persons with a standard of living superior to his own and grows envious. Thus the members of society disregard the general welfare in favor of their personal interests, so that the conditions making for the *virtue* which is the foundation of the republic are lacking. But this very diversity of the component parts makes for cohesion. The ambition that fosters rivalry among classes and individuals also leads them to perform their particular functions as well as possible. They therefore work unconsciously for the common good, though to their own minds they are promoting only their personal interests.

Emulation results in a harmony between the different elements of society.

Montesquieu calls this stimulus to public life in a monarchy *honor*. He uses the term to designate the particular ambitions of individuals or classes which make men strive to attain as high a status as possible. Such an attitude is possible only if men have a certain concern for dignity and freedom. Thus *honor* is not without its greatness, but it may give rise to excessive self-love and can easily become a failing. In several passages, Montesquieu speaks with a certain severity of *honor* and of monarchic customs in general. However, he does not mean to disparage monarchy. These shortcomings spring solely from the development of private enterprise and the greater freedom enjoyed by individuals in the pursuit of their interests. *Virtue*, to his mind, is so rare and difficult to attain that the prudent ruler will use it with the utmost caution. This wise organization of society, which without requiring virtue impels men to great undertakings, is so admirable in Montesquieu's opinion, that he readily forgives it certain imperfections.

I shall say little of despotism, for Montesquieu himself seems to have been less concerned with it. This form of government stands midway between the societies we have been discussing. A despotism is either a variety of monarchy in which all the orders have been abolished and there is no division of labor, or a democracy in which all the citizens except the ruler are equal, but equal in a state of servitude. Thus it has the aspect of a monster, in which only the head is alive, having absorbed all the energies of the organism. The principle of social life in such a society can be neither *virtue*, because the people do not participate in the affairs of the community, nor *honor*, because there are no differences of status. If men adhere to such a society, it is from passive submission to the prince's will, that is, solely from *fear*.

The foregoing suffices to make it clear that Montesquieu distinguished definite types of society. This would be still more evident if we went into detail, for they differ not only in structural principles but in all aspects of life. Customs, religious practices, the family, marriage, the rearing of children, crimes and punishments, are not the same in a republic, a monarchy, and a despotism. Montesquieu seems even to have been more interested in the differences between societies than their similarities.

[III]

The reader may wonder why, if Montesquieu actually classified and described types of society, he defined and named them as he did. He distinguishes them and names them, not on the basis of division of labor or the nature of their social ties, but solely according to the nature of the sovereign authority.

These different points of view are not incompatible. It was necessary to define each type in terms of its essential property from which the others follow. At first sight, the form of government seems to meet this condition. No aspect of public life is more apparent, more evident to all. Since the ruler is at the summit, so to speak, of society and is often, not without reason, referred to as the "head" of the nation, everything is thought to depend on him. Furthermore, Montesquieu's predecessors had not yet discovered any other aspect of social phenomena that could serve as a principle of classification, and despite the originality of his approach it was hard for him to break entirely with their point of view.

This explains why he classified societies according to form of government. To be sure, this method is subject to many objections. The form of government does not determine the nature of a society. As we have shown, the nature of the supreme power can be modified while the social structure remains unchanged, or conversely it can remain identical in societies which differ in the extreme. But the error lies in the terms rather than the realities, for apart from the political regime Montesquieu mentions many other characteristics by which societies can be differentiated.

If we overlook his terminology, we shall probably find nothing more truthful or more penetrating in the entire work than this classification, the principles of which are valid even today. The three forms of social life he described constitute three really distinct types, and he gives a fairly accurate account of their specific natures as well as the differences between them. Of course there was not quite so much equality and frugality in the ancient city-states as Montesquieu supposed. But it is true that in these societies the scope of private interests was more limited and the affairs of the community occupied a larger place than in modern nations. Montesquieu had an admirable understanding of the fact that the individual citizen of Rome and Athens had very few personal possessions and that this made for social unity. In modern society, on the other hand, individual life has a wider field. Each of us has his own personality, opinions, religion, and way of life; each one draws a profound distinction between himself and society, between his personal concerns and public affairs. Hence social solidarity cannot be the same, nor can it spring from the same source; it results from the division of labor, which makes the citizens and the social orders dependent upon each other. With great insight, Montesquieu distinguishes what he calls despotic government from the other types of organization, for the Persian and Turkish empires had nothing in common with the Greek and Italic cities or with the Christian nations of Europe.

It may be argued, however, that despotic government is merely a form of monarchy, for even in a monarchy the king has the right to modify laws, so that his will is the supreme law. But the structures of these societies are quite different. The differences of status peculiar to monarchy do not exist in the despotic state. In a monarchy, moreover, it is unimportant whether or not the king has the right to modify the laws; in actual practice he cannot do so because his power is limited by the power of the orders. The justified objection has been raised that no despot has ever held unlimited power. But Montesquieu himself corrects his earlier definition and recognizes that even in a despotic state there are checks upon the sovereign power, though they are different from those that operate in a monarchy, having their source not in the power of the various orders, but in the supreme and unrivaled authority enjoyed by religion not only among the people but also in the mind of the despot. Beyond a doubt religion has such power in these societies. It is not only independent of the prince's will, but as Montesquieu pertinently observes, it is the source of his exorbitant power. Thus it is not surprising to find that religion limits his power.

For a clear understanding of Montesquieu's view of

this subject, we must add a fourth type of society, one which his commentators tend to overlook but which requires our attention for it is the source of monarchy. It consists of the societies that live by hunting or cattle raising. These differ from the others in many important ways. For example, their population is very small; land is not divided among the members; they have no laws, but only customs; the elders have supreme authority but are so jealous of freedom that they tolerate no lasting power. Unquestionably these are characteristics of inferior societies—one might classify them as inferior democracies. Montesquieu divides this type into two categories: when men live dispersed in small societies having no social tie between them, he calls them *savages;* when they live in societies united to form a larger whole, he calls them *barbarians*. The former are generally hunters; the latter are cattle raisers.

Montesquieu's classification of societies is set forth in the following table:

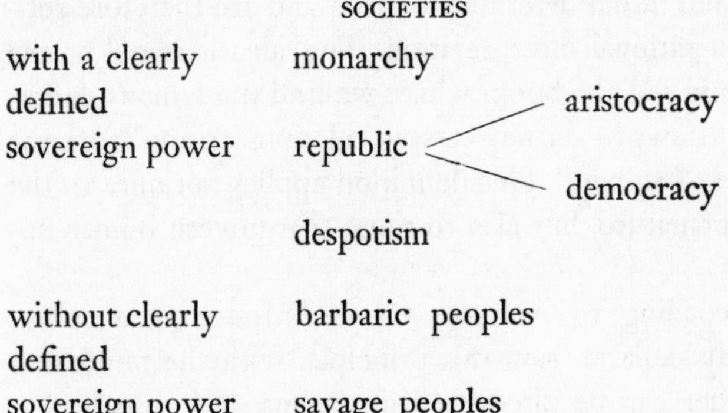

One has only to consider this table and the wide variety of peoples it covers to see that Montesquieu did not simply take over Aristotle's classification with slight changes, but produced an original system.

To What Extent Did Montesquieu Believe That Social Phenomena Are Subject to Definite Laws?

[I]

Montesquieu does not confine himself to classifying societies. He believes that social phenomena, especially those with which he is particularly concerned, namely, laws, fall into a determinate order and are therefore subject to rational interpretation. This idea is stated at the beginning of the book, where we find the famous definition: "Laws . . . are necessary relations arising from the nature of things." This definition applies not only to the laws of nature, but also to those that govern human societies.

According to Auguste Comte, Montesquieu subsequently departs from this principle, with the result that no order can be discovered in the mass of facts he has accumulated.[9] This accusation is unfounded. Whenever Montesquieu formulates a law, he shows that it depends upon definite conditions. These are of two kinds: first those inherent in the nature of the things to which the law pertains, for example, to the nature of trade if it pertains to trade, to that of religion if it concerns religion; and secondly, the more far-reaching and important conditions inherent in the nature of the society involved. As we have already said, most laws cannot be the same in a monarchy as in a republic or despotic state. Among inferior peoples laws do not exist at all. Given the type of state, the system of laws must follow.

Montesquieu follows the causal sequence still further. Not content to show that the laws depend upon the form of the society, he seeks out the causes upon which the form of society itself depends and, among these causes, the one that plays the major role, that is, the volume of the society.

Let us, for example, consider a society confined within narrow limits. The affairs of the community are at all times present to the eyes and mind of every single citizen. Since the conditions of existence are approximately the same for all—for in such a society the mere lack of space makes diversity impossible—the way of life is much the same for everyone. Even those who are in power are only *primi inter pares*, for they have been invested only with a limited authority consonant with the limits of the society. Always present to the minds of all, the thought of their country has great force because it is not limited by any other. This is clearly a description of the republic. But if the society grows larger, everything changes. It becomes more difficult for the individual citizen to have a sense of the public weal, for he perceives only a small part of the country's interests. The increasing differentiation of society gives rise to divergent outlooks and objectives. Further, the sovereign power becomes so great that the person who exercises it is far above all others. The society cannot but change from the republican to the monarchic form. But if the volume increases still further and becomes excessive, monarchy gives way to despotism, for a vast empire cannot subsist unless the prince has the absolute power enabling him to maintain unity among peoples scattered over so wide an area. So close is the relationship between the nature of a society and its volume that the principle peculiar to each type ceases to operate if the population increases or diminishes excessively.

Of course, a number of objections are in order at this point. Many nations whose population is limited or even quite small are ruled by despots. Others, such as the Jewish nation, whose population was far larger than those of the Greek and Italic cities, had a certain form of democratic organization. And if we look into the details we often find something rather vague and uncertain in the explanation itself. Nevertheless, Montesquieu displays great insight in attributing such influence to the number of social units. This factor is indeed of the highest importance in determining the nature of societies, and in our opinion accounts for the chief differences between them. Religion, ethics, law, the family, etc., cannot be the same in a large society as in a small one. There is one point, however, which Montesquieu failed to note, namely that the essential is not the number of persons subject to the same authority, but the number bound by some kind of relationship. For however large the number of persons who obey the same leader, if the distance between groups is so great that there can be little or no relation between them, the size of the population produces no effect.

Montesquieu mentions several other factors affecting the nature of societies, and it is on these that the commentators have focused their attention. For example, there is the geographical character of the territory. Broad, unbroken plains favor the establishment of a despotic state because great empires can spread more easily in country of this sort. Mountainous regions and islands, on the other hand, are citadels of freedom because mountains and the sea are obstacles to a leader's authority. Not only the topography, but also the nature of the soil must be taken into consideration. A barren soil makes for industry and thrift, which open the way to the republic. A fertile soil, on the other hand, makes for self-interest and love of wealth and conduces to monarchy. An excessively fertile soil makes for the inferior forms of democracy, for since it is naturally productive, it does not have to be cultivated, hence divided among the members of the group. Lastly, a warm climate enervates mind and body and forces men into servitude.

These factors partially determine not only the nature of a society and its general legal structure, but even the substance of particular laws. Thus, an extremely hot climate gives rise to civil slavery, polygamy, and certain domestic customs. The resulting listlessness of mind and body makes for the immutability of laws, religious practices, and customs. This explains why trade is so different in the Orient and in Europe.

Although Montesquieu does not put topography and climate in the same rank as size of population and although he recognizes that they are dominant only among savage peoples, it must be admitted that their influence has nowhere been so great as he thought. Domestic, political, and private virtue is to be found in countries which differ completely in climate and soil. Yet even this exaggeration shows how strongly Montesquieu felt that social phenomena are subject to definite laws.

What has been said thus far may be summarized as follows: a country's type of society, laws, and institutions can be deduced from the size of its population, its topography, climate, and soil.

But we have discussed only one part of the doctrine set forth by Montesquieu in *The Spirit of Laws*. Let us now turn to another, which seems to be at variance with the first. The contradiction should be examined very closely, for it will enable us to obtain a better understanding not only of our author's ideas, but also of the difficulties encountered by the development of social science not only in Montesquieu's time but in our own as well.

[II]

As we have seen, once we grant that there is a determinate order in social existence, we necessarily reduce the role of the lawgiver. For if social institutions follow from the nature of things, they do not depend upon the will of any citizen or citizens. In Montesquieu's work, however, the lawgiver emerges as the indispensable maker of the laws. In numerous passages he speaks of the laws of Rome, Sparta, and Athens as though they had been created out of whole cloth by Romulus, Numa, Solon, and Lycurgus. When, in another work, he relates the early history of the Roman state, he puts forward the principle that the institutions of new nations are created by the leaders and that only thereafter are the leaders shaped by the institutions. It is for this reason that he distinguishes sharply between laws and customs: customs spring spontaneously from social existence; laws are established by the spontaneous will of the lawgiver. Such is the implication of the following statement in the first chapter of the book: "Formed to live in society, he might forget his fellow creatures; legislators have therefore . . . confined him to his duty." Of course Montesquieu did not believe that laws could be made arbitrarily; he held that customs and religion were beyond the power of the lawgiver and that even laws relating to other matters had to be compatible with customs and religion. But the actual establishment of these laws is in the hands of the lawgiver. There are even societies in which not only the laws but the religion and customs as well can, to some extent, be fashioned by the prince. Though this rarely occurs, the statement shows how much importance Montesquieu attaches to political authority.

This we shall readily understand if we ask what Montesquieu meant by his statement that human laws spring from the nature of things—for it can be interpreted in two ways. It may mean that the laws follow from the nature of things—that is, of societies—as an effect follows from the cause that produces it; or else it may mean that they are simply instruments that the nature of the society requires in order to fulfill itself, that is, to attain its ends. Are we, in other words, to understand that the state of society is the efficient cause of the laws or only their final cause? Montesquieu does not even seem to suspect the possibility of the first of these meanings. He does not say that the laws of a democracy result necessarily from the limited number of its citizens as heat results necessarily from fire, but rather that they alone make possible the frugality and general equality which are in the nature of this kind of society. Nor does it follow from this that the laws can be framed arbitrarily, for, under given social conditions, only one body of laws is appropriate and no other can be imposed on a society without vitiating it. But what is suitable to a particular society can be ascertained only by men who have insight into its nature and are capable of indicating what objective it should strive for and by what means. That is the task of the lawgivers. Thus it is not surprising that Montesquieu should accord them a certain primacy. If we assume, however, that the laws are produced by efficient causes of which men may often be unaware, the function of the lawgiver is reduced. Then it consists merely in expressing with superior clarity what is dimly perceived by the minds of others. But the lawgiver produces nothing—or next to nothing—that is new. Even if he did not exist, there would have to be laws, though they would be less sharply defined. However, he alone can frame them. Granted. But he is only the instrument of their promulgation, not their generating cause.

This is not the place to discuss whether there are social institutions that depend entirely upon final causes. In any case, we can be certain that there are very few. Social life embraces so many phenomena that no mind is capable of reckoning with them all. Hence it is no easy matter to foresee what will be useful and what harmful. Even if such calculation were not, for the most part, beyond the powers of the human mind, it would be so abstruse as hardly to influence men's deliberate actions. Social phenomena are not, as a rule, the product of calculated action. Laws are not devices that the lawgiver thinks up because they seem to be in harmony with the nature of the society. They spring most often from causes which engender them by a kind of physical necessity. In consequence of the society's particular situation, communal life must necessarily assume a certain definite form. This form is expressed by the laws, which thus result with the same inevitability from the efficient causes. To deny this is to assume that most social phenomena, particularly the most important, have no cause whatsoever. The laws suitable to Roman society could never have been deduced from the small size of early Rome. The equality and frugality, which according to Montesquieu were imposed by the laws, were not created by these laws. They resulted from a way of life and were merely consolidated by the laws.

Montesquieu would doubtless have seen this had he recognized that laws do not differ in nature from customs but on the contrary derive from them.[10] They are simply customs more sharply defined. As everyone knows, customs are not created deliberately but are engendered by causes that produce their effects quite unbeknownst to men. The same applies to the origin of most laws. This does not mean that they are useless. Quite the contrary. They could not remain in force if they did not perform certain useful social functions. But it was not this utility that brought them into being. Far from deliberately striving for it, men have generally been quite unaware of it. We feel that the rules of law and custom are good, but if we were asked what purpose they served, the discussion would be endless. Though we may understand how a given law is useful to society, this does not explain its origin. Hence anyone who limits his inquiry to the final causes of social phenomena, loses sight of their origins and is untrue to science. This is what would happen to sociology if we followed Montesquieu's method.[11]

[III]

The rules of law do not follow necessarily from the nature of a society, since they remain hidden in the depths of reality unless some lawgiver discerns them and brings them to light. And moreover, according to Montesquieu, they can even take a form other than that resulting from the causes which produce them. He ascribes to human societies some sort of ability to deviate from their own nature. To his mind, men do not observe the natural laws inherent in their makeup with the same necessity as inanimate things, and can at times shake off their yoke. Montesquieu thus introduces into social phenomena an element of contingency which seems, at first sight at least, irreconcilable with the existence of a determinate order since, where such contingency prevailed, the relation between cause and effect would cease to be constant and immutable. It is essential that we define this contingency, for there is reason to fear that it may destroy the very foundations of social science.

It might be supposed that Montesquieu put forward this principle because he thought it indispensable to the concept of human freedom. But if this were the true reason, the contingency would admit of no exception and would extend to all of life. We would not expect our author, who says so definitely that men and societies are governed by laws which he sets out to ascertain, to contradict himself in such a way. Moreover, it seems quite unlikely that his view was based on any metaphysic. Nothing in his entire work suggests the slightest concern with metaphysical problems. Nowhere does the question of free will arise. Consequently there is no reason to suppose that a philosophical hypothesis should assume such importance for him. And there is a passage in the first chapter of the book which runs distinctly counter to such an interpretation. Here Montesquieu states that this element of contingency is not peculiar to man. He also finds it in animals, and even the plants do not seem entirely devoid of it.

He tells us that he himself conceived it only as a means of explaining the origin of error. If we never made mistakes, we should obey the laws of nature under all circumstances. If we wish to find out what led him to this opinion, we must first determine what he means by the "nature of things." In using this term he refers, not to all the properties of a thing, but only to those which encompass the others and determine the species to which the thing belongs; in short, its *essence*. Moreover he believes that there is a logical tie between the nature of a thing and its normal forms, the latter being implicit in the former. Thus, if it is true that men and societies never deviate from their nature, they will always and everywhere be what they must be. But both individual life and social life are in many ways imperfect. There are unjust laws and faulty institutions stemming from mistakes of the lawmakers. As Montesquieu sees it, all this seems to indicate that man has a certain faculty for deviating from the laws of nature. This is no justification for speaking of facts without causes. But these causes are fortuitous and, as it were, "accidental." Hence they cannot be reduced to laws; they corrupt the nature of things, which the laws on the contrary express.

The principle on which this whole line of argument depends is certainly false. In so far as these errors have to do with social existence, they are simply diseases of the social organism. But disease no less than health is inherent in the nature of living things. The two states are not contraries. They belong to the same type. They can therefore be compared, and the interpretation of both benefits from such comparison. But this false opinion fits in so well with the outward appearance of things that it held its ground for a long time, even in psychology. Since it seemed evident that living things were naturally healthy, it was concluded that disease is a violation of the state of nature because it is an obstacle to health. Thus Aristotle believed that disease, monsters, and all wayward forms of life were the result of some obscure contingency. It was not possible to rid social science of this error all at once, particularly since disease is nowhere so prevalent as in human societies and since the normal state is nowhere else so indeterminate and difficult to define.

This accounts for several passages in which Montesquieu seems to attribute to the lawgiver the strange power of doing violence to nature itself. For example, in countries where excessive heat inclines the inhabitants to sloth, he enjoins the lawmaker to repress such laziness in every possible way. But although this vice springs from physical causes, Montesquieu does not think that to oppose it is to violate the laws of nature, but rather that it represents a striving to lead men back to their normal nature, which is incompatible with such indolence. For the same reason, he says that in societies of proud and fearless people severe punishments should be employed to check their ardor. If the lawmaker has such power in all these cases, it is not because the societies are without laws or definite nature and can therefore be organized however he wishes, but rather because his action is in keeping with the normal nature of men and societies, which it merely serves to abet.

Thus Montesquieu's point of view implies no actual contradiction. He does not say that a determinate order exists or is lacking in respect to the same social facts. Wherever things are normal, they follow necessary laws, and this necessity ceases only when there is a deviation from the normal state. Consequently, the element of contingency does not destroy social science, but only limits its scope. Social science is concerned almost exclusively with the normal forms of life in society; in Montesquieu's opinion, diseases are virtually beyond the scope of science, because they are not subject to the laws of nature.

Even his conception of natural law, which is fundamental to all his ideas, remains very obscure and imprecise. Laws are the necessary relations between things, but if they can sometimes be violated, the necessity is no longer real but purely logical. In this event they will express what is implied in the definition of a society, but perhaps the definition will not follow rationally from the nature of the society in question. Then they will tell us what is rational rather than what actually exists. And indeed, though Montesquieu, far from thinking that men always or even frequently deviate from the straight path, shows a kind of spontaneous respect for what has been confirmed by prolonged general experience, he nevertheless recognizes that all the individuals of an identical species disclose certain anomalies. He fails to see that whatever is uniformly present in an entire species cannot but correspond to definite necessities. For example: although the institution of slavery existed in all the Greek and Italic cities, he says it is repugnant to the nature of republics. Although only men enjoy the right to repudiate their spouse in societies where women live under a regime of domestic slavery, he insists that in these same societies the contrary should be true. He even goes so far as to say that only one type of society is inherently defective and corrupt, namely despotism, although he recognizes that it is necessary in certain places. Under such circumstances the order that science should seek would be different from anything that has ever existed. Consequently the laws that express it can only have an ideal form, for they express what ought to be rather than what is. These laws are not, like the other laws of nature, inherent in phenomena, or rather they are not the phenomena themselves considered under a particular aspect; they are above the phenomena, though their authority is not always respected.

In this regard, Montesquieu reverts, to a certain extent—but only to a certain extent—to the older conception of social science. Sometimes, to be sure, he is not far from confusing natural laws with rules prescribing proper conduct. But he is far from following in the footsteps of the ancient philosophers who ignore nature as it is and set up another nature of their own. Though formulating no exact principle to that effect, he understood instinctively that a thing can rarely be universal unless it is healthy and rational at the same time. That is why he attempted, as we have seen, to describe and explain social types on a historical basis. He did not venture to correct them until he discovered something that struck him as inconsistent with their essence as he conceived it from his observation of reality. Although Montesquieu's conception of natural law does not extend to the whole of social existence, it is applicable to the greater part of it. If his work retains some of the old confusion between art and science, something vague and uncertain, this defect is only occasionally apparent.

Montesquieu's Method

[I]

So long as social science was only an art, writers on social questions chiefly employed the deductive method. From the general notion of man they derived the form of society consonant with human nature and the precepts to be observed in social life. There is need to dwell on the shortcomings of this method. Even in art, deduction provides only simple hypotheses. If a rule has not been tested by experience, it is not possible to establish its utility by reason alone. Particularly in science—as distinguished from art—the role of deduction can only be secondary, at least when we are dealing with realities and not with abstract notions as in mathematics. Of course deduction offers us ideas that guide us amid the obscurities of experience, but unless these ideas are confirmed by observation, we cannot tell whether they actually express the reality. The only way to discover the laws of nature is to study nature itself. Moreover, it is not enough to observe nature. She must be questioned, hounded, put to the test in a thousand and one ways. Since social science deals with phenomena, it can achieve its objectives only through the experimental method.

It is not easy to adapt this method to social science, because it is impossible to experiment with societies. However, there is a way around this difficulty. In order to discover the laws of nature, one need only make a sufficient number of comparisons between the various forms of a given thing. In this way, the constant, unchanging relations expressed in the law are distinguished from those that are merely ephemeral and accidental. The essence of experimentation is simply to vary phenomena freely, so that they offer a broad and rich field for comparison. But there is no objection to comparing social phenomena of the same class as they appear in different societies and noting those which always tally, those which disappear simultaneously, and those which vary at the same time and in the same proportions. Although it is not possible to make such comparisons over and over, they can nevertheless meet the need for experiment in social science.

Though Montesquieu did not discuss the matter, he instinctively recognized the necessity of this method. His purpose in gathering a large body of data from the history of various nations was to compare them and derive laws from them. Indeed, his entire work is clearly a comparison of the laws observed by the most divergent peoples, and it is perfectly correct to say that in *The Spirit of Laws* Montesquieu instituted a new field of study, which we now call *comparative law*.

But although deduction cedes to experience in his work, it still plays a greater role than science permits. In his preface, he informs the reader that he intends to deal with social science in an almost mathematical way, that he lays down principles from which the particular laws of societies follow logically. He realized, of course, that such principles must be derived from the observation of reality, but he believed that all science is implicit as it were in such observation, so that once the principles have been derived, the edifice can be completed by pure deduction. There is no doubt that he tried to proceed along these lines.

Let us first examine his way of using the inductive method. He does not begin by marshalling all the facts relevant to the subject, by setting them forth so that they can be examined and evaluated objectively. For the most part, he attempts by pure deduction to prove the idea he has already formed. He shows that it is implicit in the nature or, if you will, in the *essence* of man, society, trade, religion, in short, in the definition of the things in question. Only then does he set forth the facts which in his opinion confirm his hypothesis.[12] But if we believe that the relations between things can be shown only by experiment, we cannot subordinate experiment to deduction. We cannot give primacy to arguments that we mistrust and regard as relatively useless for purposes of demonstration. We first observe the phenomena and only afterwards interpret deductively what we have observed.

If we examine Montesquieu's own demonstrations, it is easy to see that they are essentially deductive. True, he usually substantiates his conclusions by observation, but this entire part of his argumentation is very weak. The facts he borrows from history are set forth briefly and summarily, and he goes to little pains to establish their veracity, even when they are controversial.[13] He lists them haphazardly. If he asserts that there is a causal relation between two facts, he does not trouble to show that in all or at least most cases they appear simultaneously, disappear simultaneously, or vary in the same way. He is content to adduce a few examples that correspond roughly to the assumed law. Sometimes he even endows an entire type with a property that he has observed only in a single society. Take for example, the matter of separation of powers. Although it is to be found only in England, he calls it the essential characteristic of monarchy, and goes on to say that freedom is a consequence of this separation, although he does not know whether freedom really exists among the English themselves. In short, instead of using deduction to interpret what has been proved by experiment, he uses experiment to illustrate the conclusions of deduction. Once the deduction has been effected, he assumes that the demonstration is as good as complete.

Let us examine the matter further. As we have seen, Montesquieu believed that there are certain institutions which, though they exist or have existed in various societies, are nevertheless unsuited to these same societies. But such an assertion can be based on only one consideration, namely that to his mind these institutions cannot be derived from the principles he has already set forth. He shows that the institution of slavery conflicts with the definition of a republic. Similarly, he detests despotic government because it is in logical conflict with the essence of man—and even of society—as he conceives it. In certain cases deduction thus prevails over observation and experiment.

Although induction made its first appearance in social science with Montesquieu, it was not yet clearly separated from the opposite method and was contaminated by the mixture. Though Montesquieu pointed the way to a new trail, he himself was unable to leave the beaten paths.

This methodological ambiguity is a consequence of the doctrinal ambiguity to which we have referred. If the normal forms of society are implicit in the nature of society, they can be deduced from a definition of the nature of society. It is these logical necessities that Montesquieu calls laws. In view of this kinship between phenomena and human reason, reason suffices for the interpretation of phenomena. It may seem surprising that this inner nature of phenomena should be so clearly apparent that it can be recognized and defined in the earliest stages of a science, for one would normally expect such insight only in a science that had attained maturity. But such a conclusion is quite consistent with Montesquieu's principles. Just as the connection between social phenomena and the essence of society is a rational one, so this essence, which is the source of the entire deduction, is also of a rational nature; that is, it consists in a simple notion that reason can grasp at one quick glance. Montesquieu did not fully realize to what extent, as Bacon says, the subtlety of things exceeds the subtlety of the human mind. This accounts for his enormous confidence in reason and deduction. We are not saying that social phenomena as such are illogical. But though they may have a certain fundamental logic, it is not the logic to which our deductive reasoning conforms. It has not the same simplicity. Perhaps it observes other laws. If we are to learn this logic, we must consult the things themselves.

The confusion of which we are speaking has still another cause. We have seen that the laws of society can be violated. Hence they cannot be arrived at solely through observation or even comparison of phenomena. Realities are not necessarily rational, but laws are rational in every respect. That is why even if something is proved by history, we cannot be absolutely sure it is true. All societies of the same kind have certain defects; it is therefore impossible to describe the normal form of these societies on the basis of what we find in them. If we cannot obtain a faithful view of phenomena through experience, experience alone cannot teach us what follows from the nature of the phenomena. There remains but one way out. We must try to attain that essence itself, define it, and from the definition infer what it implies. From this we must not conclude that observation is useless, but rather that it must be suspect until it is confirmed by reason and that if by chance it cannot be so confirmed, it must be rejected. We see how indispensable it is in social science to discover in the data themselves some definite indication enabling us to distinguish between sickness and health. If such a sign is lacking, we are driven to take refuge in deduction and move away from the concrete facts.

[II]

Whether he proceeds by deduction or induction, Montesquieu observes a methodological rule that modern science ought not to overlook.

Social phenomena are usually classified according to considerations which might appear at first sight to be wholly unrelated. Religion, law, morality, trade, and administration seem indeed to differ in nature. This explains why each class of phenomena was long treated separately—and sometimes still is—as though it could be examined and explained by itself, without reference to the others, just as physicists do not take color into consideration when dealing with weight. It is not denied that one class of phenomena is related to the others, but the relationships are regarded as merely incidental, so that, since the inner nature of the phenomena cannot be ascertained, it seems safe to disregard the relations between them. For example, most moralists deal with morality and rules of conduct as though they existed by themselves, and do not bother to consider the economic character of the societies in question. Those who deal with the subject of wealth maintain in like manner that their science, namely, political economy, is absolutely autonomous and can carry on without the slightest attention to the system of rules that we call ethics. One could give many such examples.

Montesquieu, however, saw quite clearly that all these elements form a whole and that if taken separately, without reference to the others, they cannot be understood. He does not separate law from morality, trade, religion, etc., and above all he does not consider it apart from the form of society, which affects all other social phenomena. Widely as they may differ, all these phenomena express the life of a given society. They are the elements or organs of the social organism. Unless we try to understand how they harmonize and interact, it is impossible to know their functions. We shall even fail to discern their natures, for they will seem to be distinct realities, each with its independent existence, whereas they are actually parts of a whole. This attitude accounts for certain errors that are still current among social scientists. It explains why many political economists have regarded personal interest as the only principle of society and why they have denied the legislator's right to interfere in activities related to trade and industry. Conversely, though for the same reason, moralists have generally regarded property rights as fixed and immutable, whereas they actually depend upon extremely varied and unstable economic factors.

This error had to be dispelled before social science could develop or even come into being. The various disciplines dealing separately with different categories of social phenomena did indeed prepare the way for social science; it was from them that it developed. But social science in the strict sense came into being only when it was clearly perceived that the branches above-mentioned were bound together by strict necessity and were parts of a whole. But such a conception could not arise until it was realized that all happenings in society are related. In pointing to the interrelatedness of social phenomena, Montesquieu foreshadowed the unity of our science—though his view of the matter was still vague. Nowhere does he say that the problems he deals with might form the subject matter of a definite science embracing all social phenomena and having a method and name of its own. And yet, without suspecting this implication of his endeavors, he gave posterity a first sample of such a science. Although he did not deliberately draw the conclusions implicit in his principles, he paved the way for his successors, who, in instituting *sociology*, did little more than give a name to the field of study he inaugurated.

[III]

Yet there is a notion of which Montesquieu seems to have been unaware, which in our time has transformed the method of social science, namely the notion of *progress*. Let us see what it means.

When we compare different peoples, it appears as

though certain forms or properties which are manifestly inherent in the nature of societies are merely adumbrated among some peoples and stand out more clearly in others. Some societies are small and dispersed over large areas; others are large and dense. Some have no firmly established authority; others have a systematically organized state administration that makes its influence felt throughout the social organism. Between these two types there are countless intermediate variations. In respect to organization, these societies are not all of the same rank so to speak. Some may be regarded as superior to others. But it has been noted that superior societies spring from inferior societies. Of course I do not mean to say that societies form a single linear series rising from the ancient peoples at the bottom to the modern nations at the top. One is reminded more of a tree with branches spreading in different directions. But this has little to do with our subject. It is nonetheless true that societies issue from other societies and that the later are superior to the earlier. This is what is meant by the progress of mankind. The same observations may be made if we consider a single people by itself. From the moment it comes into being it rises little by little above the type from which it sprang. The progress of human nature consists of these little cumulative developments.

Yet Montesquieu failed to see this. True, he does not put all societies on the same level. He preferred the republic and monarchy to despotism, monarchy to the republic, and the republic to the democracy of barbaric peoples. But he did not suspect that these different kinds of society grow successively from the same root. He thinks that each springs up independently of the others, except for monarchy which, he believes, develops out of the inferior democracy.[14] But this very exception shows how far he is from the idea of progress, since primitive democracy, which he regards as superior to no other form of society,[15] is for him the original type precisely because it is inferior to all others. For the same reason, though he does not deny that the social principle of particular peoples can be developed or corrupted, he nevertheless believes that this principle is determined when a people comes into existence, and must be preserved intact throughout its history. He fails to see that every society embodies conflicting factors, simply because it has gradually emerged from a past form and is tending toward a future one. He fails to recognize the process whereby a society, while remaining faithful to its nature, is constantly becoming something new.

This accounts for the singularity of his method.

Social existence is determined by conditions of two types. One consists of present circumstances, such as topography or size of population. The other pertains to the historical past. Just as a child would be different if he had had other parents, so the nature of a society depends upon the form of the societies preceding it. If it has a background of inferior societies, it cannot be the same as if it had sprung from highly civilized nations.

Failing to see the relations of succession and kinship between societies, Montesquieu completely overlooks causes of this kind. He does not reckon with this *vis a tergo* that drives societies forward, but considers only environmental factors.[16] When he attempts to interpret the history of a society, he does not situate it in a series of societies, but concerns himself only with the nature of its topography, the number of its citizens, etc. This is utterly contrary to the method adopted later by Comte in dealing with the same problem. Comte holds that the nature of a society depends entirely upon the time of its emergence and that social science consists almost entirely in establishing the series of societies. Needless to say, neither of these doctrines expresses more than a part of the truth.

Conclusion

In his history of political philosophy, Paul Janet, after setting forth Montesquieu's theory, rightly complains that most commentators have been interested only in exposing its errors. He adds that it would have been preferable and much fairer "to have given a detailed idea of the vastness and obscurity of the subject he chose and of the intellectual power with which he mastered it."[17] This is what we have tried to do in the present work. We have not discussed Montesquieu's opinions in matters of detail, but dwelt only upon what struck us as his major achievement. Although it is always a mistake to trace the birth of a science to a particular thinker—since every science is the product of an unbroken chain of contributions and it is hard to say exactly when it came into existence—nevertheless, it is Montesquieu who first laid down the fundamental principles of social science.[18] Not that he stated them in explicit terms. He speculated very little about the conditions of the science he inaugurated. But these principles and conditions are inherent in his ideas, and it is not difficult to recognize and formulate them.

We have seen what they are. Not only did Montesquieu understand that social phenomena are matter for scientific study; he also helped to shape the two fundamental ideas necessary for the establishment of social science, namely the ideas of *type* and of *law*.

In regard to *type*, Montesquieu shows that the nature of the sovereign power and of social existence in general differs from one society to another, but that the different forms can nevertheless be compared. This is an indispensable condition for classification; it is not enough that societies should manifest similarities of one kind or another; it must be possible to compare them in their whole structure and existence. Montesquieu not only formulated principles, but also used them with great skill. His rough classification contains a considerable element of truth. But he was mistaken in two points. First, he erroneously assumes that social forms are determined by the forms of sovereignty and can be defined accordingly. Second, he states that there is something intrinsically abnormal about one of the types he distinguishes, namely, the despotic state. Such a view is incompatible with the nature of a type, for each type has its own perfect form which—allowances being made for conditions of time and place—is equal in rank to the perfect form of the other types.

As for the notion of *law*, it was more difficult to transfer it from the other sciences in which it was already established to ours. In all sciences the notion of type appears earlier than that of law, because the human mind conceives it more readily. One has only to look around to note certain similarities and differences between things. But the determinate relations we call laws are closer to the nature of things and consequently hidden within it. They are covered by a veil that we must first remove if we are to get at them and bring them to light. In regard to social science, there were certain special difficulties resulting from the very nature of social existence, which is so mobile, diversified, and rich in forms that to my mind it cannot be reduced to fixed and immutable laws. Moreover, men do not like to think that they are bound by the same necessity as other natural phenomena.

Nevertheless, despite appearances, Montesquieu maintains that social phenomena have a fixed and necessary order. He denies that societies are organized haphazardly and that their history depends on accidents. He is convinced that this sphere of the universe is governed by laws, but his conception of them is confused. According to him, they do not tell us how the nature of a society gives rise to social institutions, but rather indicate the institutions that the nature of a society requires, as if their efficient cause were to be sought only in the will of the lawgiver. He also applies the word laws to relations between ideas rather than between things.[19] To be sure, these ideas are those which a society must hold if it is faithful to its nature, but it can depart from them. Yet his social science does not degenerate into pure dialectics because he realizes that what is rational is precisely what exists most often in reality. Thus his ideal logic is to some extent situated in the empirical world. But there are exceptions which introduce an element of ambiguity into his concept of law.

Since Montesquieu all social science has endeavored to dissipate this ambiguity. No further progress could be made until it was established that the laws of societies are no different from those governing the rest of nature and that the method by which they are discovered is identical with that of the other sciences. This was Auguste Comte's contribution. From the notion of law he eliminated all the foreign elements that had hitherto falsified it, and he rightly insisted on the primacy of the inductive method. Only then could our science become fully aware of its objective and method. Only then was its indispensable groundwork complete. The present study will enable the reader to judge Montesquieu's contribution to this groundwork.

Rousseau's *Social Contract*[1]

The chief objective of *The Social Contract*, as presented in Book I, Chapter 1, may be stated as follows: to find a form of association, or, as Rousseau also calls it, of *civil state*, whose laws can be superimposed upon the fundamental laws inherent in the *state of nature* without doing violence to them. In order to understand Rousseau's doctrine, we must accordingly: 1) determine what he means by his "state of nature," which serves as a kind of yardstick by which to measure the degree of perfection attained by the "civil state"; 2) determine how men came to depart from this condition when they founded societies, for if the perfect form of society remains to be discovered, we must conclude that reality offers no model. Only then shall we be in a position to examine Rousseau's reasons for believing that this deviation was not inevitable and his remarks as to how the two states, at variance in several respects, can be reconciled.

The State of Nature

The *state of nature* is not, as has sometimes been said, the state in which man lived before societies came into being. The term might indeed suggest a historical period at the beginning of human development. This is not what Rousseau meant. It is, he says, a state "which exists no longer, which perhaps never existed, which probably never will exist" (Preface to *Discours sur l'origine de l'inégalité*). Natural man is simply man without what he owes to society, reduced to what he would be if he had always lived in isolation. Thus the problem is more psychological than historical, namely, to distinguish between the social elements of human nature and those inherent in the psychological makeup of the individual. In the state of nature, man consists solely of the latter elements. In order to determine what he was "when he emerged from the hands of nature," we must strip him "of all the supernatural gifts he may have received and of all the artificial faculties he can have acquired only through long progress" (*ibid.* and Part I). If, as assumed by Rousseau, Montesquieu, and nearly all thinkers up to Comte (and even Spencer relapses into the traditional confusion), nature ends with the individual, then everything that goes beyond the individual is bound to be artificial. Rousseau does not ask whether man remained in the state of nature for any considerable time or began to deviate from it as soon as he came into being, for the question is irrelevant to his purpose.

Consequently, history is of no use to him, and he quite legitimately disregards it. "Let us begin by disregarding all facts, for they have no bearing on the question. All investigations of the matter should be taken not as historical truths but as hypothetical, conditional speculations, *more likely to shed light on the nature of things than to reveal their actual origin*" (*ibid.*, beginning, *in fine*). Even the savages give a very inaccurate idea of the state of nature. "Many thinkers have been mistaken about man's primitive tendencies and have, for example, credited him with a native cruelty, because they did not sufficiently realize how far these peoples [the savages] were already removed from the first state of 'nature.' The savage is doubtless closer to nature. In his mental state, it is no doubt easier in many respects to discern the original background, because it is less hidden by the acquisitions of civilization. But by now it is a debased image which must be examined with great caution." How then are we to proceed? Rousseau has no illusions about the difficulties of his undertaking. "A satisfactory solution to the following problem would seem to me not unworthy of the Aristotles and Plinys of our century. What experiments should we require in order to know the natural man, and by what means can we conduct such experiments for the benefit of society" (*ibid.*, Preface)? Such experiments are impossible. What techniques can be substituted? Rousseau does not state them explicitly, but the principal methods would seem to be: 1) observation of animals, which furnish examples of mental life uninfluenced by society; 2) observation of savages, with the aforementioned reservation; 3) a kind of dialectic aimed at deducing all the mental factors that seem to be logically implied by subsequent social developments (such as language).

Why did Rousseau proceed in this way? Why does he make the theory of the state of nature, as thus defined, the basis of his system? Because, as he replies, this primitive condition is "the root" of the civil state. "If I have dwelt at such length on the supposition of this primitive condition, I have done so because, having ancient errors and inveterate prejudices to destroy, I thought it necessary to dig down to the root" (*ibid.*, Part I). It seemed obvious to him that society could only be a concretization of the characteristic properties of the nature of the individual. It is therefore from the individual nature that we must start and to it that we must return. In order to judge the historical forms of association, we must examine them in relation to human nature, trying to ascertain whether they follow from it logically or whether they deform it. And when we seek to determine what form should replace them, an analysis of natural man must provide the premises of our reasoning. But in order to arrive at this natural man, we must put aside everything within us that is a product of social existence. Otherwise, we should find ourselves in a vicious circle, for we should be justifying society on the basis of society, that is, of the ideas and feelings society has implanted in us. We should be demonstrating one prejudice by another. If we wish to proceed both critically and effectively, we must break away from the action of society and dominate it; we must start from the origin and review the logical sequence of things. This is the aim of the operation we have just described. Rousseau's constant preoccupation was to avoid "the error of those who, in reasoning about the state of nature, make use of ideas drawn from society" (*ibid.*, Part I). To this end, we must rid ourselves of all preconceptions of social origin, whether true or false, or, as he puts it, "clear away the dust and sand surrounding the edifice" and "discover the solid foundation on which it stands" (*ibid.*, Preface, *in fine*). This solid foundation is the state of nature.

One cannot fail to be struck by the resemblance between this method and that of Descartes. Both thinkers hold that the first operation of science should be a kind of intellectual purge that will clear the mind of all mediate judgments that have not been demonstrated scientifically and lay bare the axioms from which all other propositions should be derived. Both set out to remove the rubble and uncover the solid rock on which the entire structure of knowledge should rest; in the one case theoretical knowledge, in the other practical knowledge. Rousseau's conception of a state of nature is not, as has sometimes been thought, a figment of sentimental reverie, a philosophical restoration of the ancient belief in the golden age. It is a methodological device,[2] although, in applying this method, Rousseau may have distorted the facts to make them more consonant with his personal feelings. In any event it springs, not from an overly optimistic view of primitive man, but from a desire to establish the basic components of our psychological makeup.

Once the problem was stated in these terms, how did Rousseau solve it? Wherein, to his mind, does the state of nature consist?

What characterizes man in this state—whether real or

ideal is of no importance—is a perfect balance between his needs and the resources at his disposal. Why? Because natural man is reduced exclusively to sensations. "The more one ponders the question, the greater seems the distance between pure sensations and even the simplest knowledge; it is impossible to conceive how a man could have bridged so great a gap by his own resources" (*ibid.*, Part I). Rousseau was led to this proposition by two considerations: 1) the example of animals, which have only sensations but think nonetheless: "Every animal has ideas, since it has senses"; 2) Condillac's theory—which he accepted—concerning the origin of general, abstract knowledge, namely, that it is impossible without language; but language is a product of social life. Hence we can safely reject all ideas about the state of nature that presuppose a system of articulated signs.

Our natural man can desire only the things to be found in his immediate physical environment, for he cannot imagine any other. Hence his desires will be purely physical and extremely simple. "His desires do not go beyond his physical needs; in all the universe the only desirable things he knows are food, a female, and rest" (*ibid.*). He does not even worry about insuring the satisfaction of his future appetites. His purely sensory knowledge does not enable him to anticipate the future; he thinks of nothing beyond the present. "His plans extend barely to the end of the day." Hence his notorious improvidence. But such needs are easily satisfied. Nature has provided for them. It is very unusual for the things he needs to be lacking. Harmony is achieved spontaneously. Man has all he desires because he desires only what he has. "Since he desires only what he knows and knows only what it is in his power to possess . . . his soul is perfectly tranquil and his mind extremely limited." Even if the products of civilization were made available to him, they would leave him indifferent, for they can have no value outside the civilization that creates them. Let us suppose that in some miraculous way a god had offered primitive man the art of agriculture and implements for tilling the soil. What would he have done with them? What would be the point of tilling the soil if property were not safeguarded, if the fruits of his labor were not protected? But the actual *institution* of a sanctioned right to property presupposes society. Under these circumstances, in short, man is in harmony with his environment because he is a purely physical being, dependent on his physical environment and nothing else. The nature within him necessarily corresponds to the nature without. One is a reflection of the other. Conditions that might make for discord are wholly lacking.

Under these circumstances, what will be the relation between human beings? There will not be a state of war. Rousseau rejects the theory of Hobbes whom he often rebukes sharply, though he praises his genius. The hypothesis of the state of war is unacceptable to Rousseau for two reasons: 1) The incentive to war, namely, unsatisfied needs, is lacking. Since man has what he needs, why should he attack others? Hobbes arrived at his system only by endowing natural man with the complex sensibility of civilized man. 2) Hobbes erroneously refused to grant that primitive man could feel pity. Since this virtue precedes all reflection, there is no reason to deny its existence in the state of nature. Besides, there are signs of it in animals. Pity merely implies an identification "of the beholding animal . . . with the suffering animal." But it is evident that such identification must have been infinitely closer in the state of nature than in a state of reason.

Some commentators have seen a contradiction between this passage and the following one from the *Essai sur l'origine des langues* (chap. 9): "How are we moved to pity? By going out of ourselves, by identifying ourselves with the sufferer . . . Think of the acquired knowledge that such outgoing implies! How shall I imagine sufferings of which I have no idea? How shall I suffer at seeing another suffer . . . if I do not know what he and I have in common? A man who has never reflected can be neither kind nor compassionate." "This," he says in the same essay "is why men did not know themselves to be brothers and thought they were enemies . . . knowing nothing, they feared everything; they attacked in self-defense." As this essay was written after the *Discours sur l'origine de l'inégalité*, critics have wondered whether Rousseau's thinking had not changed, moving toward Hobbes and his theory of the state of war. But this interpretation is invalidated by the following statement that appears in the same chapter: "Those barbaric times were the golden age . . . the entire earth was at peace." All that Rousseau means in the controversial passage is that in order to see a man, a fellow creature, in every human being, one must have powers of abstraction and reflection that primitives lack. For them, mankind is limited to their immediate entourage, the small circle of individuals with whom they have relations. "They had the idea of a father, son and brother, but not of man. Their hut contained all their fellow creatures . . . apart from these and their family, the universe meant nothing to them" (*ibid.*). Actual pity was therefore possible only in this small circle. "Hence the apparent contradictions we observe among the brothers of the nations . . . so fierce in their ways and so tender-hearted; such love of family and such aversion to their kind." Thus he does not repudiate the notion that pity is a sentiment natural to man and preceding reflection. He simply points out that reflection is necessary before compassion can extend to all mankind. The *Essai* may be regarded as at most a clarification and partial correction of the idea developed in the second *Discours*. In any case, he definitely continued to reject Hobbes' pessimism about presocietal man. Limited as the range of pity may then have been, there was no war, for men did not come into contact: "Perhaps, if you will, men attacked each other when they met, but they seldom met. The state of war reigned everywhere, and the earth was at peace" (*ibid.*).

But even if man is not a wolf to his fellow men, it does not necessarily follow that he is inclined to unite with them permanently and form societies in the strict sense of the word. He has neither the means nor the need to do so. He lacks the means because his intelligence, limited to momentary sensations, having no conception of the future, cannot even imagine what such an association—of which he has no visible example—might be. The absence of language suffices in itself to make social relations impossible. And moreover, why should he aspire to such an existence? His desires are satisfied. He cannot covet what he does not have. "It is impossible to imagine why, in this primitive state, a man should need another man any more than a monkey or wolf should need another of its kind" (second *Discours*, Part I). It is said that man must have been utterly wretched in such a state. But what matter, if he was so constituted by nature that he had no desire to change? Besides, the word "wretched" is meaningless unless it implies painful privation. But what is a man deprived of if he lacks nothing, if "his heart is at peace and he is sound of wind and limb"? Does the savage complain of his existence and seek to change it? It could make him unhappy only if he had an idea of another state and if, in addition, the other state appeared to him in a highly attractive light. But "thanks to a wise providence, his potential faculties developed only when there was occasion to exercise them." He had only instinct, and instinct sufficed him; it did not lead him to social existence. In order to live in society, he needed reason, which is the instrument of adaptation to the social environment, as instinct is the instrument of adaptation to the physical environment. It came eventually, but in the beginning it was only virtual.[3]

We must therefore conceive natural man as "wandering through the forest, without occupation, without speech, without a home, without war and without ties, with no need of his fellow men and no wish to harm them, perhaps not even recognizing any of them individually." At that stage of his development, he was not unsocial, but asocial. "He is not hostile to society, but has no inclination toward it. He has within him the seeds which, if nurtured, will develop into social virtues, social inclinations, but they are only potentialities. *Perfectibility*, the social virtues and other faculties that were potential in natural man, could never have developed by themselves" (second *Discours*, end of Part I). Similarly, man in this condition is neither moral nor immoral; he is amoral. "Since men in this state had no kind of moral tie between them and no known duties, they could be neither good nor bad and had neither vices nor virtues" (*ibid.*). Morality could come into being only with society. Rousseau frequently refers to this state as the state of innocence.

Is such a state the most perfect ideal that men can set up for themselves? In relation to the determinate conditions to which it corresponds, it is perfect of its kind. So long as these conditions do not change—assuming that they ever obtained fully in a general and durable way—nothing could be better, since the harmony between the human being and what we would now call his environment leaves nothing to be desired. In other words, so long as man has relations only with the physical environment, instinct and sensation suffice for all his needs. He can desire nothing else, and there is nothing to awaken the various aptitudes that lie dormant within him. Consequently, he is happy. But if things change, the conditions of his happiness cannot remain the same. It is such changes that gave rise to care. Something must have upset the existing balance, or, if it was never really stable, certain factors must have marred it from the very beginning. What are these factors?

Origin of Societies

There comes a point, says Rousseau in *The Social Contract*, "at which the obstacles in the way of their [men's] preservation in the state of nature show their power of resistance to be greater than the resources at the disposal of each individual for his maintenance in that state. That primitive condition can then subsist no longer; and the human race would perish unless it changed its manner of existence" (I, 6, beginning). To explain the genesis of societies is to find these forces conflicting with the state of nature. Rousseau recognizes that this problem can be dealt with only by conjecture, for, he says, "the events to be described could have occurred in many ways" (second *Discours*, end of Part I). But while these conjectures are quite plausible since they follow logically from the definition of the state of nature, a detailed knowledge of what happened has little bearing on the consequences that may be derived from the system.

Society can come into existence only if man is prevented from remaining in the state described above. But this requires an external cause. Since the only environment that affects him is his physical environment, it is there that the cause must be sought. If the earth had always satisfied his needs, it is hard to see how the state of nature could ever have come to an end. "Imagine a perpetual springtime on earth. Imagine human beings emerging from the hands of nature and strewn about in such a setting. I cannot see how they would ever have surrendered their primitive freedom and given up their isolated existence, so appropriate to their natural indolence" (*Origine des langues*, IX). Rousseau supports this belief by pointing out that "the mild climates and fertile lands were the first to be inhabited and the last in which nations were formed" (*ibid.*). But the resistance men encountered in nature stimulated all their faculties. "Barren years, long, severe winters, torrid, all-consuming summers that demanded new effort." The cold gave them the idea of wearing the skins of the animals they had killed; thunder and volcanoes added to the necessity of protecting themselves against wintry temperature, gave them the idea of preserving fire; and so on. And so intelligence began to develop beyond sensation. New needs arose. The balance was beginning to be upset.

Before long it became evident that the help of others was useful in satisfying these new and more complex needs. "Having learned from experience that the love of well-being was the sole motive of human action, he was able to distinguish the rare occasions on which common interest obliged him to count on the help of his fellows" (second *Discours*, Part II). Thus were formed the first loose-knit herds of human beings. Their coming together was facilitated by a host of circumstances which are mentioned in detail in the *Essai sur l'origine des langues*:

"Floods, tidal waves, volcanic eruptions, earthquakes, fires caused by lightning, which destroyed forests, whatever was bound to frighten and scatter the savage inhabitants of a region brought them together to join in repairing the damage suffered in common."—"Springs and rivers, unequally distributed, were other meeting-points that were particularly necessary, since men could do without water still less than fire" (*Essay*, IX). "Out of this first human intercourse grew the beginnings of language. A common idiom was bound to arise among men thus brought together and forced to live side by side rather than among those who freely roamed the forests" (second *Discours*, Part II).

Thus a first extension of physical needs creates a slight tendency to form groups. Once these groups are organized, they in turn arouse social inclinations. And once men have got used to being together, they find it hard to live alone. "They grew accustomed to gathering together. Having begun to see one another, they could no longer dispense with seeing one another." This gave rise to new ideas about human relations, the need for civility, the duty of respecting contractual obligations. An embryonic ethics came into being. It was approximately at this point that the savages ceased to be savages.

But mankind went further. As men emerged from their original indolence, as their faculties were sharpened by more active relations, their minds opened to new ideas. Some discovered the principle of agriculture, from which the other arts derived. The idea of using fire in agricultural activities occurred quite naturally. This gave rise to the first division of labor, on the one hand metallurgy, on the other the plowing and cultivation of the soil. Farming necessitated the partition of land. From the recognition of property the first rules of justice were born. The way now lay open to all kinds of inequalities. In the state of nature, men differed very little from one another, and there was nothing to make them accentuate and develop their differences. But now rewards awaited those who could produce most and best. New-found desires led to competition. "Thus, hand in hand with the progress of combination natural inequality spread imperceptibly; the differences among men, developed by differences of circumstance, became more apparent and more permanent in their effects, and began to exert a parallel influence on the lot of individuals" (*ibid.*).

But as soon as there began to be rich and poor, powerful and weak, "the beginnings of society gave way to the most terrible state of war. Debased and ravaged, unable to retrace its steps or give up its unfortunate acquisitions, the human race had reached the brink of ruin" (*ibid.*). Thus the state of war is not, as Hobbes thought, the origin, but rather an effect, of the social state. Before men could conceive the idea of seeking, at one another's expense, a happiness beyond what they already possessed, a first association must have unleashed their passions, broadened their intelligence, in short, upset the original balance. Once this calamity befell mankind, the rich man, who was the most severely affected because he had the most to lose, conceived "the most astute project that has ever occurred to the human mind, namely the idea of employing to his own advantage the very power of those who attacked him, of turning his opponents into his defenders." With this intention, he proposed to his fellows that they institute rules of peace and justice to which everyone would have to conform, that all individual forces be united into one supreme power which would protect and defend all the members of the association. Thus were laws and governments established.

Such are the origins of the civil state. If we consider

the terms in which Rousseau envisaged the problem, we cannot fail to admire the dialectical ingenuity with which he handled it. He starts with the individual and, without ascribing to him the slightest social inclination or conflicting tendencies such as might tend, through the evils to which they gave rise, to make society necessary, he undertakes to explain how a being so fundamentally indifferent to any kind of life in common came to form societies. It is as though, in metaphysics, after assuming the subject to be self-sufficient, we should attempt to deduce the object from it. The problem is obviously insoluble, and we may be sure in advance that Rousseau's solution is fraught with contradictions. But it is far from specious. In order to grasp what follows, we must bear in mind the instability of the original balance. We must not forget that though social life does not exist in the beginning, its germs are present. They are embryonic, but if favorable circumstances arise, they cannot fail to develop. Man does not yet feel a need to perfect himself, but he is already perfectible. It is this perfectibility, says Rousseau, that most distinguishes him from the animal (second *Discours*, Part I). He is not like the animal, which is unable to change. His intelligence and sensibility are not circumscribed by fixed moulds. Latent within him is an element of instability that the merest trifle can bring into play. If he is not to vary, the environment must remain stationary and invariable, or rather, everything in the environment must correspond to the organization of nature, and nothing must happen to disturb it. Once the balance is upset, it cannot be restored. One disorder follows from another. Once the natural limit is crossed, there is no turning back. Passions beget passions and stimulate the intelligence, which offers them new objectives that rouse them to a fever pitch. The very satisfactions they obtain make them more demanding. "Superfluity awakens cupidity. The more one has, the more one wants" (fragment entitled *Distinction fondamentale*, from the Neufchâtel manuscripts, ed. Dreyfus-Brisach, p. 312). Men come to need each other more and more and become increasingly interdependent. Thus they emerge *naturally* from the *state of nature*.

Although the formula seems self-contradictory, it expresses Rousseau's thinking. Let us try to understand it.

It is natural causes that lead man gradually to form societies. But this does not make society a natural phenomenon, for it is not logically implicit in the nature of man. It was not man's original constitution that constrained him to enter into social life, the causes of which are outside of human nature, adventitious. Rousseau even goes so far as to say that they are fortuitous, that they might very well not have been. "Having shown that the social virtues could never have developed unaided, that their development required the fortuitous aid of several foreign causes which might never have arisen and without which man would have remained eternally in his primitive state, I must now consider and compare the various chance occurrences that have brought man and the world to their present state" (second *Discours*, Part I, *in fine*). Society comes into being because men need each other. This mutual assistance is not *naturally* necessary. Each individual can be self-sufficient. Thus, in order for society to arise, external circumstances must increase man's needs and consequently modify his nature.

But there is still another reason for saying that society

is not natural. It is artificial to a still higher degree. Not only is the interdependence that is the prime mover of social evolution not rooted in human nature, but even when it begins to exist it is not in itself sufficient to make societies. To this original base, which is itself a product of human art, must be added something else, that has the same origin. Until this intercourse is regulated and organized in a definite way, it does not constitute a society. It lacks the "connection between the parts, that constitutes the whole" (*Manuscrit de Genève*, ed. Dreyfus, chap. II, p. 248). A society is "a moral entity having specific qualities distinct from those of the individual beings which compose it, somewhat as chemical compounds have properties that they owe to none of their elements. If the aggregation resulting from these vague relationships really formed a social body, there would be a kind of common sensorium that would outlive the correspondence of all the parts. Public good and evil would not be merely the sum of individual good and evil, as in a simple aggregation, but would lie in the relation that unites them. It would be greater than that sum, and public well-being would not be the result of the happiness of individuals, but rather its source" (*ibid.*, p. 249). But the mere fact that men realize that they can help each other and have fallen into the habit of doing so, even when added to the feeling that they all have something in common, that they all belong to the human race, does not form them into a new kind of corporate body with its own specific character and composition, that is, a society. Thus "it is certain that the human race suggests a purely collective idea which does not presuppose any real union of the individuals composing it."

This remarkable passage proves that Rousseau was keenly aware of the specificity of the social order. He conceived it clearly as an order of facts generically different from purely individual facts. It is a new world superimposed on the purely psychological world. A conception of this kind is far superior even to that of such recent theorists as Spencer, who think they have grounded society in nature when they have pointed out that man has a vague sympathy for his fellow men, and that it is to his interest to exchange services with them. Feelings of this kind may make for momentary contacts between individuals, but these intermittent and superficial relationships which, as Rousseau puts it, lack the "connection between the parts, that constitutes the whole," are not societies. Rousseau realized this. In his view, society is nothing if not a single definite body distinct from its parts. He says elsewhere that "the body politic, taken individually, may be regarded as a live, organized body, similar to that of man. The sovereign power represents the head . . . the citizens are the body and limbs which make the machine move and work and injury to any part of which carries a painful sensation to the brain if the animal is in good health" (*Economie politique*). However, since only the individual is real and natural, the whole can only be a product of reason. "The body politic is only a product of reason" (fragment from *Distinction fondamentale*, p. 308). Individuals create it, and since they remain the matter and substance of the construction, it can never attain the same degree of unity and reality as a work of nature: "The difference between human art and the work of nature can be felt in their effects. It is all very well for the citizens to call themselves the limbs of the state; they cannot unite as real limbs unite with the body. It is impossible to prevent each one from having an individual and separate existence and attending to his own needs" (*ibid.*, p. 310). Rousseau was unaware that there are natural organisms whose parts have this same individuality.

Not only the body politic, but the family as well, is a product of reason. It is indeed a natural group in so far as the children are attached to their parents by the need for self-preservation. But this need lasts only a certain time. Once the child is able to look after himself, he remains with his parents only if he so desires. There is nothing in the nature of things that obliges him to retain his association with them. "If they remain united, they continue so no longer naturally, but voluntarily" (*Social Contract*, I, 2). But it follows from many passages that this association by mutual agreement was the first to be formed. In fact, Rousseau seems at times to regard it as contemporaneous with the most primitive state.

In short, every society is an artificial entity because man has no natural need of it and because it is essentially an organized body and because there are no social bodies among the natural bodies. These two ideas, which we customarily regard as conflicting—the conception of society as a product of reason and the conception of society as an organism—are both to be found in Rousseau. And he does not pass from one to the other by any conscious or unconscious development that he might have tried to conceal from his readers and perhaps even from himself. No, the two ideas are closely related in his mind. One seems to imply the other. It is because society is an organism that it is a work of art, for, from this point of view, it is superior to individuals, whereas in nature there is nothing beyond the individual. Formulated in these terms, the theory may very well seem self-contradictory. It may seem more logical to say that if there is something above individuals, there is something outside them. Every attempt to widen the circle of natural phenomena requires a great effort, and the mind resorts to all kinds of subterfuges and evasions before resigning itself to so grave a change in its system of ideas. Is there any less contradiction in the writings of Spencer, who on the one hand regards society as a product of nature, a living thing like other living things, and on the other strips it of its specific character by reducing it to a mechanical juxtaposition of individuals? Rousseau attempts at least to solve the problem without abandoning either of the two principles in question, the individualist principle (which underlies his theory of the state of nature as well as Spencer's theory of natural law) and the contrary principle (which might well be called the socialist principle if the word did not have a different meaning in the language of political parties), which is at the base of his organic conception of society. As we shall see, the coexistence of these two principles explains the dual aspect not only of Rousseau's social philosophy, which might be called his sociology, but also of his political doctrines.

But need we go further? Granting that society is not in nature, must we conclude that it is contrary to nature, that it is and can be only a corruption of human nature, the consequence of some sort of fall and degeneration; in short, that society as such is an evil that can be reduced but not eliminated?

A distinction must be made. Society as it is today is certainly a monstrosity that came into being and continues to exist only through a conjunction of accidental and regrettable circumstances. Social development has led to artificial inequalities that are utterly contrary to those inherent in the state of nature. Natural or physical inequality is that which "springs from a difference of age, health, physical strength, and mental and spiritual qualities. The other inequality which may be called moral or political, depends on a kind of convention . . . [It] results from the various privileges enjoyed by some to the detriment of others, such as the privilege of being richer, more highly respected, more powerful" (second *Discours*, beginning). These conventions invest individuals or groups of individuals who, in the state of nature, would not be superior and might even be inferior to others, with exceptional power which confers upon them a superiority contrary to nature. "It is manifestly contrary to the law of nature, however we may define it, for a child to order an old man about, for a fool to guide a sage, and for a handful of people to be glutted with superfluity while the hungry multitude lacks the bare necessities of life" (second *Discours*, last lines). These inequalities result chiefly from the social convention known as inheritance. In the state of nature, inequality hardly exists. Its development is stimulated by social evolution, and "it becomes stable and legitimate through the establishment of property and laws."

The first violation of the law of nature led to a second. When men became unequal, they became dependent upon each other. Consequently society is composed of masters and slaves. The masters themselves, in a sense, are the slaves of those they dominate. "A man thinks he is master of others, whereas he is actually more of a slave than they" (*Social Contract*, I, 1). "Domination is itself servile when it rests on public opinion" (*Emile*, II), for one becomes dependent on the prejudice of those whom one governs with prejudices. This interdependence of human beings is contrary to nature. Men are naturally independent of each other. Such is the meaning of the famous statement: "Man is born free, and everywhere he is in chains." In the natural state, he depends only upon nature, the physical environment, that is, upon impersonal and invariable forces which are not controlled by any individual but which dominate all individuals alike.

The impersonality of the physical forces and the regularity of their action are certainly, in Rousseau's opinion, signs by which we can distinguish what is normal and justified from what is abnormal and accidental. To his mind, what is good should have a certain degree of necessity. Hence one of the reasons why he regards the present social state as morbid is its extreme instability. As soon as men enter into relations, "there arise a multitude of vague, formless relationships that men are continually deforming and changing; for every individual who tries to stabilize them, a hundred do their best to destroy them" (*Manuscrit de Genève*, ed. Dreyfus, chap. II, p. 247). We might add the following passage from *Emile*: "All things are mingled in this life. One does not remain in the same state for two consecutive moments. The affections of the mind and the modifications of the body are in perpetual flux" (II). For the wills of individuals move in different directions and consequently conflict. Now one prevails, now another. They enter into combination, one yields to the other, but always in different ways, the balance is forever being upset. "There are two kinds of dependence, dependence on things, which is a phenomenon of nature, and dependence on men, which is a social phenomenon. Dependence on things is not an obstacle to freedom and does not breed vice; but since the dependence of men upon men is without order or stability it breeds every vice; and it is through this dependence that the master and the slave deprave each other" (*Emile*, II). When man depends only upon things, that is, upon nature, he necessarily lives in a state of stable equilibrium, since his needs are in harmony with his means. Order is achieved automatically. Man is then truly free, for he does whatever he desires because he desires only what is possible. "The truly free man desires only what is possible and does as he pleases" (*ibid.*).

Thus freedom, as conceived by Rousseau, results from a kind of necessity. Man is free only when a superior force compels his recognition, provided, however, that he accepts this superiority and that his submission is not won by lies and artifice. He is free if he is held in check. However, the energy that holds him must be real and not a mere fiction like that developed by civilization. It is only on this condition that he can desire to be dominated. And Rousseau adds: "If the laws of societies, like those of nature, became so inflexible that no human force could ever bend them, dependence upon men would become dependence upon things" (*ibid.*).

But if the civil state as it is now violates the law of nature, will the same be true of every civil state? Is the present evil necessarily implicit in all social organization, or is it rather an error that can be corrected? Are the state of nature and life in society irreducibly antithetical, or is there some way of reconciling them?

Rousseau has often been credited with the opinion that perfection was possible for human beings only in a state of isolation, that they were doomed to corruption and degeneration as soon as they began to live together, that the golden age is a thing of the past, which vanished forever when we departed from the *sancta simplicitas* of primitive times, and from which we move further and further away the more we become involved in the tangle of social ties. From this point of view, *The Social Contract* becomes unintelligible, for if society as such is an evil, our sole concern with it should be an endeavor to reduce its development to a minimum, and we are at a loss to understand all Rousseau's effort to provide it with a positive organization. Particularly the importance he attaches to collective discipline and his subordination, in certain respects, of the individual become quite inexplicable.

Rousseau certainly prefers the state of nature to the civil state that he sees about him, for in its way it is a state of perfection. Perhaps he expresses himself violently at times, and we may be tempted to wonder whether his diatribes are meant for modern societies only or for society in general. In view of the difficulties involved in the social adventure, we can understand how he may have deplored the circumstances that put an end to the isolation of primitive man. But there is no ground for supposing that he regarded this state of perfection as the only possible state of perfection and thought it impossible to define and establish another, different in kind but equal in value. One reason for not imputing to Rousseau the radical pessimism that has been attributed to him is that the germ of social existence is inherent in the state of nature. The original equilibrium could have been maintained indefinitely only if man had been unwilling to accept any change, if he had not been perfectible. But what distinguishes him most from the animal is "the ability to perfect himself. This ability which, with *the help of circumstances*, successively develops all the other faculties, is characteristic of the species as well as the individual" (second *Discours*, Part I).

It is true that perfectibility remains dormant in the natural man until it is awakened by the circumstances. Even so, it is latently present from the very start, and the series of events that proceed from it cannot be regarded as necessarily contrary to nature, since it exists in nature. These events may take an abnormal turn, but such a turn is not predetermined by their causes. Similarly, reason, which is to the social environment what instinct is to the physical environment, was awakened in man by Providence (second *Discours*). Hence social existence is not contrary to the providential order.

Although the present civil state is imperfect, it does have qualities not to be found in the state of nature. Though natural man is not evil, he is not good; morality does not exist for him. If he is happy, he is not aware of being so. "The dull creatures of primitive times are unaware of" their felicity (ed. Dreyfus, p. 248). Although Rousseau (in the second *Discours*) stresses the sufferings caused by civilization in its present form, he does not close his eyes to its grandeur, but seems merely to doubt whether this is sufficient compensation. "It seems advisable to suspend the judgment we might pass on such a situation until, after weighing one thing against another, we have determined whether the progress of their knowledge is sufficient compensation for the harm they do one another as they come to know more and more" (Part I). But then, if there is some way of correcting these imperfections or making them impossible, the grandeur alone will remain, and perhaps this new perfection will be superior to that of the original state. The fact remains, of course, that such perfection will have been acquired at the cost of great suffering, but Rousseau does not seem to have asked whether the price will have been too high. However, the question is beside the point, for the circumstances that make society necessary are given and the hypothetical perfection of the state of nature is consequently impossible.

Rousseau declared, as early as the second *Discours*, that the present defects of the civil state are not necessary. How then can society be organized in such a way as to make us better and happier? The purpose of *The Social Contract* is to answer this question.

The Social Contract and the Establishment of the Body Politic

Let us first see how, in the light of what has been said, Rousseau states the problem.

When the circumstances that prevent man from remaining in the state of nature have developed beyond a certain point, they must, if man is to survive, be neutralized by opposing circumstances. A system of counterforces must be established. Since these forces are not given in the state of nature, they must be provided by man. "But as men cannot engender new forces, but only unite and direct existing ones, they have no other means of preserving themselves than the formation, by aggregation, of a sum of forces great enough to overcome the resistance. These they have to bring into play by means of a single motive power, and cause them to act in concert. This sum of forces can arise only where several persons come together" (*Social Contract*, I, 6). From this it follows that, once the state of nature has become impossible, a *constituted society* is the only environment in which man can live.

But if, in the process of formation, society does violence to man's nature, the evil that has been avoided will be replaced by no less an evil. Man will live, but he will be unhappy since his mode of existence will be in constant conflict with his basic tendencies. This new life must therefore be organized without violence to the law of nature. How is this possible?

Does Rousseau try, in some vaguely eclectic way, to superimpose upon the primitive condition a new condition that is merely added to the first but does not modify it? Does he merely juxtapose social man to a natural man who remains unchanged? This strikes him as inconsistent. "Anyone who tries to preserve natural sentiments in the social order does not know what he wants. He is constantly contradicting himself . . . he will never be either a man or a citizen" (*Emile*, I). "Good social institutions are those which are best able to alter man's nature, to take away his absolute existence . . . and to transfer the self to the community."

Thus nature and society cannot be reconciled by outward juxtaposition. Nature must be recast. Man must change completely if he is to survive in the environment he himself has created. This means that the characteristic attributes of the state of nature must be transformed and, at the same time, maintained. Hence the only solution is to find a means of adapting them to the new conditions of existence without deforming them in any essential way. They must assume a new form without ceasing to be. This they can do only if social man, though differing profoundly from natural man, maintains the same relation to society as natural man to physical nature. How is this possible?

If in present societies the relations fundamental to

the state of nature are upset, it is because primitive equality has been replaced by artificial inequalities and, as a result, men have become dependent upon one another. If instead of being appropriated by individuals and personalized, the new force born of the combination of individuals into societies were impersonal and if, in consequence, it transcended all individuals, men would all be equal in regard to it, since none would be in personal command of it. Thus they would depend, not upon each other, but upon a force which by its impersonality would be identical, *mutatis mutandis*, with the forces of nature. The social environment would affect social man in the same way as the natural environment affects natural man. "If the laws of nations, like those of nature, could be so inflexible that no human force could ever bend them, man's dependence would again be a dependence upon things. All the advantages of the natural state and of the civil state would be united in the republic. The morality that lifts man to the plane of virtue would be joined to the freedom that keeps him free of vice" (*Emile*, II). The only way to remedy the evil, he says in the same passage, is to arm the law "with a real force superior to the action of any individual will."

In a letter to the Marquis de Mirabeau (July 26, 1767) he formulates what he calls *the great problem in politics*: "To find a form of government that places the law above man."

But it is not enough that this force, which is the keystone of the social system, should be superior to all individuals; it must also be based on nature, that is, its superiority must not be fictitious but rationally justifiable. Otherwise, it will be precarious and so will its effects.

The resulting order will be unstable, lacking the invariability and necessity characteristic of the natural order. It will be unable to endure except by a combination of accidents that may cease to exist at any moment. Unless individuals feel that their dependence on the social order is legitimate, the social order will be precarious. Society must therefore have principles "derived from the nature of reality and based on reason" (*Social Contract*, I, 4). Since reason is bound to submit the order thus achieved to scrutiny from the viewpoints both of ethics and of interest, these points of view must be in harmony, for an antinomy would make the social order irrational and unstable. If there were a conflict between these two motives, it would never be possible to know which one would prevail. "In this inquiry," says Rousseau at the very beginning of the book, "I shall endeavor always to unite what right sanctions with what is prescribed by interest, in order that justice and utility may in no case be divided" (*Social Contract*, Introduction). It may seem surprising at first to find Rousseau, for whom society is not in the domain of nature, saying that the force on which society is based must be natural, that is, grounded in nature. But *natural* is here synonymous with *rational*. Even the confusion is explainable. Although society is the work of man, he fashions it with the help of natural forces. It will be natural in a sense if it uses these forces in accordance with their nature, without doing violence to them; if man's action consists in constantly combining and developing properties which without his intervention would have remained latent, but which are always present in things. This is what enables Rousseau to hold by and large that despite the difference between them the social environment is only a new form of the primitive environment.

Thus men will be able to emerge from the state of nature without doing violence to the law of nature, on condition that they unite in societies dependent upon a force or system of forces that is based on reason and dominates all individuals.

Can such a result be achieved and, if so, how? Is it sufficient that the strongest subjugate the rest of society? But his authority will be durable only if it is recognized as a right. Physical power can entail neither right nor obligation. Furthermore, if right is the handmaiden of might, it changes with might and ceases when might disappears. As might varies in innumerable ways, so does right. But a right that is so variable is not a right. Hence if might is to make right, it must have a justification, which is not provided by its mere existence (*Social Contract*, I, 3).

Grotius had attempted to give the right of the strongest a logical foundation. Starting with the assumption that an individual may alienate his freedom, he concludes that a people may do the same. Rousseau rejects this theory for several reasons: 1) Such alienation is rational only if some advantage is offered in return. The despot is said to insure the peace of his subjects. But this peace is far from complete; it is troubled by the wars that spring from despotism. Besides, peace in itself is not a good; peace may be found in dungeons. 2) The freedom of future generations may not be alienated. 3) To renounce one's freedom is to renounce one's manhood, and there is no possible compensation for such renunciation. 4) A contract which stipulates that one of the contracting parties shall have absolute authority is meaningless, for it cannot stipulate anything for the party that has no rights.

Grotius had argued that the right of war implies the right of slavery. Since the victor has the right to kill the vanquished, the latter may purchase his life with his freedom. However: 1) The supposed right to kill the vanquished remains to be proved. It is said to follow from the state of war. But between individuals there is no such thing as a chronic and organized state of war, either in civil life, where everything is governed by law, or in the state of nature, where men are not naturally enemies, where their relations are not constant enough to pass as relations of war or peace. A state that never existed cannot be invoked as the foundation of a right. War is not a relation between man and man, but between state and state. Is Grotius speaking of war between nations and the right of conquest? But war does not give the victor the right to massacre the vanquished people. It therefore cannot justify the right to enslave them. Once the defenders of the enemy state lay down their arms, the victor has no right over their lives. One has the right to kill the enemy only when one is unable to subdue him. Thus the right to subjugate is not based on the right to kill. 2) Acceptance of slavery does not put an end to the state of war. In taking from the vanquished the equivalent of life, the victor does not grant him a free pardon. He commits an act of force, not of legitimate authority (*Social Contract*, I, 4).

Even if the right of the stronger could be justified rationally, it would not provide a basis for society. A society is an organized body in which each part is dependent upon the whole and vice versa. There is no such interdependence in the case of a mob subjected to a chief. Such a mob is "an aggregation, but not an association" (*Social Contract*, I, 5). The chief's interests are different from those of the mass. That is why the multitude, which was united only so long as it depended upon him, breaks up when he dies. In order for there to be a people, the individuals composing it must be and feel united in such a way as to form a whole, whose unity depends on no external cause. Such unity cannot be achieved by the ruler's will; it must be internal. The form of government is secondary. The people must first exist before it can determine how it is to be governed. "Before examining the act by which a people gives itself to a king," it would be better "to examine that by which it has become a people." This act is "the true foundation of society" (*ibid.*).

Such an act can obviously consist only in an association. Hence the problem may be stated as follows: "Find a form of association which will defend and protect with the whole common force the person and goods of each associate, and in which each, while uniting with all, may still obey himself alone, and remain as free as before." Such an association can result only from a contract by which each member alienates himself, with all his rights, to the community.

By this contract, each individual will vanishes into a common, general will, which is the basis of the society. The force thus established is infinitely superior to the sum of the forces of all the individuals. It has an inner unity, for in entering the association the component parts have lost some of their individuality and freedom of movement. Since the alienation was effected unreservedly, no member has a right to complain. Thus, the antisocial tendency inherent in each individual simply because he has an individual will is nullified. "At once, in place of the individual personality of each contracting party, this act of association creates a moral and collective body composed of as many members as the assembly contains voters, and receiving from this act its unity, its common identity, its life and its will" (*Social Contract*, I, 6). Whether such a contract is actually drawn up and in all due form, is of no importance. Perhaps the conditions have never been stated. But in so far as society is normally constituted, they are tacitly recognized everywhere (*ibid.*).

In consequence of this contract, each personal will is absorbed into the collective will, for each man, "in giving himself to all, gives himself to nobody." This general will is not an individual will that subjugates all others and reduces them to a state of immoral dependency. It has the impersonal character of natural forces. A man is no less free for submitting to it. Not only do we not enslave ourselves by obeying it, but, what is more, it alone can protect us against actual servitude, for if, to make this will possible, we must forego subjugating others, others must make the same concession. Such is the nature of the equivalence and compensation that reestablish the balance of things. If there is compensation for the alienation of my person, it is not, as Paul Janet has said, because I receive in exchange the personality of others. Such an exchange might well seem incomprehensible. It is even contrary to the basic clause of the social contract, according to which it is the body politic as a corporate body *sui generis*, and not the individuals, which receives the persons of its members ("in our corporate capacity, we receive each member as an indivisible part of the whole"—*ibid.*). What we receive is the assurance that we shall be protected by the full force of the social organism against the individual encroachments of others. Even the concession we make is not a curtailment of our freedom, for we cannot enslave others without enslaving ourselves. "Freedom consists less in asserting one's will than in not being subject to others. It consists also in not subjecting the will of others to our own. He who is a master cannot be free" (8th *Lettre de la Montagne*). The same applies to equality. It remains as complete as in the state of nature, though it has assumed a new form. Originally it followed from the fact that each individual formed an "absolute unit"; its present foundation is that "as each gives himself absolutely, the conditions are the same for all" (I, 6). From this equality there also results a state of peace of a new kind. Since the condition of all men is the same, "no one has any interest in making it burdensome to others" (*ibid.*).

Not only have freedom and equality been preserved; in a way they are even more perfect than in the state of nature. In the first place, they are more secure because they are guaranteed not by the power of the individual, but by the forces of the collectivity which "are incomparably greater than those of an individual" (I, 9). Secondly, they have a moral character. In the natural state, each person's freedom "is bounded only by the strength of the individual" (I, 8), that is, only by the material environment. Thus it is a physical fact and not a right. In the civil state, it is limited and governed by the general will and accordingly transformed. Instead of being regarded exclusively as an individual advantage, it is related to interests that transcend the individual. The collective being—superior to all individual beings—not only determines individual freedom, but also consecrates it and so endows it with a new nature. An individual's freedom is now based, not on the amount of energy available to him, but on his obligation, deriving from the fundamental contract, to respect the general will. This is what makes individual freedom a right.

The same holds for equality. In the state of nature, each man possesses what he can. But such possession "is merely the effect of force" (*ibid.*). Although the privilege of occupancy has a firmer moral basis than the privilege of the stronger, it too becomes "a real right only when the right of property has already been established," that is, after the establishment of the civil state. Each member of the community gives himself to it with the property he possesses *de facto*. All this property together becomes the public territory. Society restores—or can at least restore—to the citizens what it has thus received. But the circumstances of this new tenure are quite different. The citizens enter into possession of their property not as private owners but "as depositaries of the public good." Usurpation is thus transformed "into a true right and enjoyment into proprietorship" (I, 9), for they are then based on each individual's obligation to content himself with what is allotted to him. "Having his share, he ought to keep to it" in order to abide by the general will (*ibid.*). "This is why the right of the first occupant, which in the state of nature is so weak, claims the respect of every man in civil society. In this right we are respecting not so much what belongs to another as what does not belong to ourselves." This, to be sure, cannot suffice to institute an equality of any kind. If society consecrated the right of occupancy without subordinating it to any rule, it would, in most cases, simply be consecrating inequality. The exercise of this right must therefore be subject to certain conditions: 1) the territory must be free at the time of occupancy; 2) an individual may occupy only as much land as he needs in order to subsist; 3) he must take possession of it not by an empty ceremony, but by labor. These three conditions, particularly the second, safeguard equality. Yet if equality becomes a right, it is not by virtue of these three principles, but essentially because the community makes it so. It is not because these three rules are what they are, but because they reflect the general will, that the equal distribution of property which follows from them is just and that the system thus established must be respected. Thus, "the fundamental compact substitutes, for such physical inequality as nature may have set up between men, an equality that is moral and legitimate" (Book I, last lines).

The transition from the state of nature to the civil state produces "a very remarkable change" in man. It results in a transformation of the *de facto* order to a *de jure* order and in the birth of morality (I, 8). The words duty and right are meaningless before society is constituted, because until then man "considered only himself," whereas now "he is forced to act on different principles." Above him is something with which he is obliged to reckon (duty) and with which his fellow men are likewise obliged to reckon (law). "Virtue is the conformity of the individual will to the general will" (*Economie politique*).[4] But it would be a serious mistake to interpret this theory as implying that ethics is based on the greater material force resulting from the combination of individual forces. This coercive power is doubtless important; it guarantees the rights that come into existence with the civil state, but it does not create them. The general will must be respected, not because it is stronger but because it is general. If there is to be justice among individuals, there must be something outside them, a being *sui generis*, which acts as arbiter and determines the law. This something is society, which owes its moral supremacy, not to its physical supremacy, but to its nature, which is superior to that of individuals. It has the necessary authority for regulating private interests because it is above them, hence not a party to disputes. Thus the moral order transcends the individual; it does not exist in material or immaterial nature, but must be introduced. However, it requires a foundation in some being, and since there is no being in nature that satisfies the necessary conditions, such a being must be created. This being is the social body. In other words, ethics cannot be inferred analytically from the facts. In order for *de facto* relationships to become moral, they must be consecrated by an authority that does not inhere in the facts. The moral order must be added to them synthetically. To effect this synthetic connection a new force is required, namely, the *general will*.

Thus it is quite unjustly that certain critics accused Rousseau of contradicting himself by condemning, on the one hand, the alienation of individual freedom for the benefit of a despot and, on the other, making such an abdication, provided it be in favor of the community, the basis of his system. If it is immoral in one case, they say, why not in the other? The reason is that the moral conditions under which it takes place are not at all the same. In the first case it is unjust because it subjects man to the power of a single individual—which is the very source of all immorality. In the latter, it places him under the authority of a general, impersonal force which governs him and, without reducing his freedom, transforms him into a moral being. The nature of the limits to which he is subject has merely changed from physical to moral. The objection springs solely from Rousseau's critics' failure to see the vast difference, from the moral point of view, between the general will and any individual will.

On Sovereignty in General

In so far as it is the source of all rights, duties and powers, the body politic instituted by the social contract is called the *sovereign.* What are the attributes of sovereignty and how does it assert itself?

Sovereignty is "the exercise of the general will." It is the collective power directed by the collective will. But what, exactly, is meant by the collective will?

The collective will is composed of all individual wills. "It must . . . come from all" (II, 4). But this first condition is not sufficient. The will of all is not, or not necessarily at least, the general will. The former "is no more than a sum of particular wills" (II, 3). The object to which all individual wills are applied must also be general. "The general will, to be truly such, must be general in its object as well as its essence . . . it must both come from all and apply to all" (II, 4). In other words, it is the product of the deliberation of the individual wills upon a question that concerns the body of the nation, upon a matter of common interest. But the word "interest" must also be properly understood.

The collective interest is sometimes conceived as the interest peculiar to the social body, which is thus regarded as a new type of personality having special needs unlike those felt by individuals. Even in this sense, to be sure, whatever is useful or necessary to society concerns individuals because they feel the effects of social conditions. But this concern is only indirect. Collective utility has a certain character of its own. It is defined, not with respect to the individual as seen from one or another point of view, but with respect to society as an organic unit. That is not Rousseau's conception of it. In his view, anything that is useful to all is useful to each. The common interest is the interest of the average individual. The general interest is that of all individuals in so far as they desire what is most appropriate, not to this or that particular person, but, in view of the civil state and the prevailing conditions of society, to each citizen. It exists as soon as "all continually will the happiness of each one" (*ibid.*). And to such a degree is the individual its object that a certain egoism is involved, for "there is not a man who does not think of 'each' as meaning him and consider himself in voting for all. . . . This proves that equality of rights and the idea of justice which such equality creates originate in the preference each man gives to himself, and accordingly in the very nature of man" (*ibid.*).

Hence, in order for the general will to manifest itself, it is not necessary or even desirable that all individual wills should join in actual deliberation, as would be indispensable if the general will were something other than the elements from which it results, for then these elements would have to be brought into contact with each other and combined before their resultant could emerge. But as it is, the ideal would be for each individual to exercise his share of sovereignty separately from the others. "If, when the people . . . held its deliberations, the citizens had no communication with one another, . . . the decision would always be good" (II, 3). Anybody intermediate between the citizens and the state cannot fail to be harmful in this respect. "It is therefore essential, if the general will is to be able to express itself, that there should be no partial society within the state, and that each citizen should think only his own thoughts" (*ibid.*). Indeed, the general will, as just defined, can be produced only by a linking of the differential characteristics of individual wills. "Take away from these same wills the pluses and minuses that cancel one another, and the general will remains as the sum of the differences" (*ibid.*). Thus, if each individual votes independently of his neighbor, there will be as many voters as there are individuals and consequently a large number of small differences, which because of their weakness will disappear in the whole. Only what hinges on no individual disposition will survive. Then the collective will tends naturally toward its proper object. But if individual groups are formed, each has its collective will, general with respect to its members but individual with respect to the state, and it is from these collective wills that the sovereign will must emerge. But precisely because these elementary wills are few in number, it will be more difficult for their differential characters to fuse. The fewer the elements that form a type, the less general the type. Here, then, the public will is in greater danger of diverging toward individual ends. If one of these groups ever becomes predominant, there remains but a single difference, "and the opinion which prevails is purely particular" (*ibid.*). In this theory we discern the horror of all particularism, the unitary conception of society, that was one of the characteristics of the French Revolution.

In short, the general will is the arithmetical mean of all individual wills in so far as their political goal is a kind of abstract self-interest. It would have been difficult for Rousseau to transcend such an ideal, for if society is founded by individuals, if they regard it only as an instrument by which to preserve themselves under particular circumstances, it can have only an individual objective. But, on the other hand, since society is not natural to the individual, who is conceived as eminently endowed with a centrifugal tendency, the social objective must be stripped of all individual character. It can therefore be only something very abstract and impersonal. Yet, in order to achieve it, one can turn only to the individual. He is the sole organ of society, since he is its sole creator. However, it is necessary to submerge him in the mass, in order to modify his nature as much as possible and prevent him from acting as an individual. Anything of a nature to facilitate individual action must be regarded as a danger. Thus we encounter at every turn the two antithetical tendencies characteristic of Rousseau's doctrine. On the one hand, society as a mere instrument for the use of the individual; on the other, the individual as dependent upon society, which far transcends the multitude of individuals.

One last comment follows from what has been said. Since the general will is defined chiefly by its object, it does not lie solely or even essentially in the specific act of collective willing. It is not itself merely because all participate in it. The assembled citizens may come to a decision which does not express the general will. "This," says Rousseau, "presupposes that all the qualities of the general will still reside in the majority; when they cease to do so, whatever side a man may take, liberty is no longer possible" (IV, 2). Hence a majority is not a sufficient condition. The individuals who collaborate in the formation of the general will must strive for the end without which it does not exist, namely, the general interest. Rousseau's principle differs from that which is sometimes invoked in an attempt to justify the despotism of majorities. If the community must be obeyed, it is not because it commands, but because it commands the common good. The common interest is not decreed; it does not exist by virtue of law; it lies outside of law, and law is what it ought to be only if it expresses the common interest. Hence the number of votes is a secondary matter. "What makes the will general is less the number of voters than the common interest uniting them" (II, 4). Long debates and heated deliberations, far from being the natural setting in which the general will is elaborated, "proclaim the ascendancy of individual interests and the decline of the state" (IV, 2). When society is in perfect health, all this complicated machinery is unnecessary for the making of laws. "The first man to propose them merely says what all have already felt" (IV, 1). In other words, the general will is not formed by the state of the collective mind at the time the resolution is passed; this is only the most superficial aspect of the matter. In order to understand it correctly, we must look beneath, into the less conscious areas, and examine the people's habits, trends, customs. Customs are "the real constitution of the state" (II, 2). The general will is thus a fixed and constant orientation of minds and activities in a definite direction, that of the general interest. It is a persistent disposition in individuals. And since the direction itself depends upon objective conditions (to wit, the general interest), it follows that there is something objective about the general interest itself. That is why Rousseau frequently speaks of it as a force operating with the same inevitability as physical forces. He even goes so far as to call it "indestructible" (IV, 1).

Sovereignty is simply the collective force—as established by the basic compact—in the service of the general will (II, 4, beginning). Now that we know the two elements from which it results, we shall have no difficulty in determining its nature:

1. Sovereignty is inalienable. This means that it cannot even be exercised by representation. "Whenever a veritable act of sovereignty is involved, the people cannot have representatives" (*Oeuvres inédites*, ed. Dreyfus, Streckeisen-Moultou, p. 47, n. 2). Sovereignty might be alienated only if the general will could be exercised through the intermediary of one or more individual wills. But this is not possible, for these two kinds of will are too different in nature and move in divergent directions. One moves toward the general, hence toward equality; the other toward the particular, hence toward preferences. The two may accidentally be in harmony for a brief time, but since such harmony does not result from their natures, it has no guarantee of permanence. The sovereign may happen to will what a certain individual wants today, but what assurance is there that this harmony will still be present tomorrow?

In short, because the collective being is *sui generis*, because it is unique of its kind, it cannot be represented by a being other than itself without ceasing to be itself (II, 4).

2. Sovereignty is indivisible. It can be divided only if one part of society decides for the rest. But the will of this privileged group is not general; consequently, the power it happens to wield is not sovereignty. The sovereign is composed of parts, but the sovereign power resulting from this composition is one. In each of its manifestations, it cannot be other than entire, for it exists only if all the individual wills enter into it as elements.

But although it is indivisible in principle, may it not be divided in its objective? On the basis of this idea, it has sometimes been said that the legislative power is one part of sovereignty and the executive another, and that these two partial powers are placed on an equal footing. But this is like saying that man is made up of several men, one of whom has eyes but no arms, another arms but no eyes, and so on. If each of these powers is sovereign, they both have all the attributes of sovereignty. They are different manifestations of sovereignty; they cannot be different parts of it.

This argument proves that the unity Rousseau attributes to the sovereign power is not organic. This power is constituted, not by a system of diverse, interdependent forces, but by a homogeneous force, and its unity results from this homogeneity. It springs from the fact that all the citizens must contribute to the formation of the general will, and they must all unite if the differential characters are to be eliminated. There is no sovereign act that does not emanate from the entire people, for if there were, it would be the act of a particular association. Now we are better able to understand what Rousseau meant by his frequent comparison of society to a living body. He did not conceive it as a whole made up of distinct parts, which work together precisely because they are distinct. His view is rather that it is or should be animated by a single, indivisible soul which moves all the parts in the same direction by depriving them, to the same degree, of all independent movement. This comparison is based on a vitalist and substantialist conception of life and society. The animal body and the social body are both actuated by a vital force whose synergic action produces the co-operation of the parts. Rousseau was certainly not unaware of the importance of the division of functions; and even in this respect his analogy holds up. However, this division of labor is for him a secondary, derivative phenomenon that does not create the unity of the individual or collective organism, but rather presupposes it. Hence, once the sovereign authority has been constituted in its indivisible unity, it can generate various organs (executive bodies) which it entrusts, under its control, with the task of implementing it. The parts which thus come into being are not parts, but emanations of the sovereign power, to which they remain subordinate, finding their unity in it and by it. Social solidarity, in short, results from the laws that attach the individuals to the group and not to each other. They are linked to each other only because they are linked to the community, that is, alienated within it. Rousseau's equalitarian individualism did not allow him to take any other point of view.

3. There is no check on sovereignty. The sovereign is not answerable to his subjects (I, 7). This is self-evident, since there is no force superior to the collective force

that constitutes the sovereign power. Besides, any check would be pointless, for "the general will is always right and tends to the public advantage" (II, 3). Indeed, the necessary and sufficient condition of the general will is that each individual desire what seems to be generally useful to all. It moves toward its end, that is, "toward the preservation and welfare of all" (*Economie politique*) as surely as the personal will of the natural man aims at his happiness and personal preservation. It may, of course, be mistaken at times. What seems to it most useful to all may not really be so. In that case, not the will but the judgment is at fault. "Our will is always for our good, but we do not always see what that is; the people are never corrupted, but are often deceived" (II, 3). "The general will is always in the right, but the judgment which guides it is not always enlightened" (II, 6). Errors occur particularly when special groups are formed within the state. If ever they gain the upper hand, their members seek what is advantageous to a given party or association or individual rather than what is advantageous to all. Private interests become dominant. However, the general will is not thereby destroyed or corrupted; it is merely "linked," that is, subordinated to individual wills. It remains unchanged and continues to move toward its natural end, but is prevented by opposing forces from acting (IV, 1).

But if there are no checks upon sovereignty, is it then unrestricted?

When the state calls upon the citizen, he should render whatever service he can. However, the sovereign should not ask the subject to make any sacrifice other than that which may be of service to all. Is there any criterion for distinguishing between legitimate sacrifices and others?

We need only refer to the preceding propositions. The general will is infallible when it is itself. It is itself when it emanates from all and is directed toward the collectivity in general. But it is false to its nature and general only in name "when it is directed to some particular and determinate object" (II, 4). It cannot pass judgment on either a man or a fact. It is competent when it passes judgment on the body of the nation indiscriminately, because the arbiter and the party to the dispute are then the same being seen from different points of view. The sovereign is the people in action; the people is the sovereign in a state of passivity. But when the sovereign will deals with an individual matter, the two terms are incongruous. On the one hand, there is the public (minus the individual concerned) and, on the other, the individual in question. Hence "the matter becomes contentious"; we cease to know "which is the judge who ought to give the decision" (*ibid.*). But the will that is exercised in such a case is no longer, strictly speaking, the general will, for it is no longer the will of the whole. The whole minus a part is no longer the whole. There is no longer a whole, but only unequal parts. What right has one to lay down the law to the others (II, 6)? (Here we have one more example of the conception by which Rousseau tries to establish a force superior to individuals, which dominates them and yet is of the same nature as they.)

Once this principle has been laid down, a limitation upon sovereignty follows naturally from it. A legitimate act of sovereignty is one in which the sovereign takes cognizance only of the body of the nation, without singling out any of its individual components. Thus it is not an agreement between superior and inferior (like slavery), but between the body and its parts, in short, between the body and itself. Any other mode of action is illegitimate. Whence it follows that, however absolute the sovereign power, it has limits. It "does not and cannot exceed the limits of general conventions" (II, 4). Consequently, however complete the self-alienation of the individual, he does not cease to preserve his rights. "Every man may dispose at will of such goods and liberty as these conventions leave him" (*ibid.*). This is what Rousseau means when, in what is only an apparent contradiction, he declares that the individuals give themselves wholly to the state, and goes on to distinguish "between the respective rights of the sovereign and the citizens" (*ibid.*).

But what if the sovereign power infringes upon these rights and exceeds these limits? According to Rousseau, it neither can nor should, for to do so, it would have to aim at an individual end and would consequently cease to be itself. When such violations occur, they are committed, not by the sovereign power but by individuals who have taken its place and usurped its authority. Hence there is no obligation to obey. (Compare with Kant.)

Of Law in General

Chapters 1 to 6 of Book II deal with the sovereign power at rest; chapters 6 to 12 consider it in motion. Rousseau shifts from the static to the dynamic. The political body has been formed; now he will describe it in action.

The act by which the sovereign will manifests itself is the law; its aim is to define the rights of each individual in such a way as to insure a balance between the parts of which society is composed. Thus they are the very objects and *raison d'être* of social organization, and Rousseau has therefore no hesitation in calling them "the source of justice and injustice in respect to the members of the state" (*Economie politique*). Not that justice can be created arbitrarily, by an act of will, as Hobbes for example thought. "What is well and in conformity with order is so by the nature of things and independently of human conventions. All justice comes from God" (II, 6). But this justice, which is immanent in things, is only virtual; it must be translated into acts. The divine law is inoperative unless it becomes a human law.

Such is the function of law, which merges with that of the sovereign; it is the supreme arbiter of individual interests. But what exactly is law? It defines itself naturally in terms of the general will, for it results from the application of all wills to the body of the nation as a whole. "When the whole people decrees for the whole people . . . a relation is then formed . . . between two aspects of the entire object . . . I call this act a law" (*ibid.*). This is further proof that fundamentally, despite Rousseau's efforts to place one above the other, there is only a difference in viewpoint between the arbiter and the parts, between the body of society and the mass of individuals.

This has several consequences: 1) The law, like the general will it expresses, can have no individual object. It may create privileges, but not confer them upon anyone in particular. This is the contrary of what Hobbes maintained: "The laws are made for Titus and Caius, and not for the body of the state" (*De Cive*, XII). The reason for this difference is that Hobbes assumed a clear line of demarcation between the sovereign authority and the multitude of subjects. The former, he held, was external to the latter and imposed its will upon each individual. The sovereign's activity was thus necessarily directed toward a person or persons situated outside it. For Rousseau, though in a sense the sovereign authority far transcends all individuals, it is only an aspect of them. When it legislates for them, it is legislating for itself, and the legislative power it exercises "resides" in them. 2) For the same reason, the law must emanate from all. It "unites universality of will with universality of object." What is ordained by one man is not a law but a decree, an executive act and not an act of sovereignty. 3) Since it is the body of the nation that legislates for itself, the law cannot be unjust, for "no one is unjust to himself" (II, 6). The general is the criterion of the just. By its nature, the general moves toward the general. It is the executives who pervert the law because they are its individual intermediaries (see 9th *Lettre de la Montagne*).

But the people itself is not competent to make the law. Although it always desires the good, it does not always know what the good is. It needs someone to enlighten it. This is the function of the legislator.

It is surprising to see Rousseau accord so much importance to the legislator, who is necessarily an individual. There seems to be a contradiction in making an individual the source of law, when the individual has been presented as the source of immorality. Rousseau is aware of this. He recognizes that human nature in itself is not equal to such a function, which requires a man who has a thorough understanding of the human heart and who, at the same time, is sufficiently impersonal to rise above human passions and individual interests. A person of this kind can only be an "extraordinary being," a kind of god, whom Rousseau postulates, so to speak, as the necessary condition for good legislation, though he has no assurance that this condition always obtains. "It would take gods to give laws to men."

The difficulty is due not only to the fact that this task requires an extraordinary genius, but also to the antinomy it implies. For to make laws involves a denaturing of human nature, a transformation of the whole into a part, of the individual into a citizen (II, 7). What powers has the legislator for performing so onerous a task? None. He can have no effective force for implementing his ideas, for if he had, he would replace the sovereign authority. Men would be commanded by an individual. However wise an individual will may be, it cannot substitute for the general will. "He who holds command over men ought not to have command over the laws." He can only propose. The people alone decides. "Thus in the task of legislation we find together two things which happen to be incompatible: an enterprise too difficult for human powers, and, for its execution, an authority that is no authority" (*ibid.*). In that case, how can he win obedience? We must bear in mind that when he undertakes the task there are still no established social customs to facilitate it. In all likelihood he will not be understood. "For a young people to be able to relish sound principles of political theory . . . the effect would have to become the cause; . . . and men would have to be before law what they should become by means of law" (*ibid.*).

In actual history legislators have been able to get around these difficulties by taking on a religious character. In the eyes of the nation the laws of the state thus acquired the same authority as the laws of nature, since both had the same origin. Men deferred to them, "recognizing the same power in the formation of the city as in that of man" (II, 7). Thus when nations come into being, religion must serve "as an instrument" of politics (*ibid.*, last lines). However, Rousseau does not mean that in order to found a society one has only to exert skill in making the oracles say the right things. A religious respect must be imposed above all by the very person of the lawmaker, by the personal genius that speaks in him. "The great soul of the legislator is the only miracle that can prove his mission." Perhaps this will enable us to understand why Rousseau regards such apotheoses as not altogether impossible even in the future.

But there are further prerequisites for good legislation. It is not enough for a legislator to guide the collective activity applying to the body of the nation. Certain conditions must also prevail among the people:

1. Once human nature is set, it can no longer be modified. The profound transformation to be effected by the legislator presupposes that man is still malleable. It is therefore possible only in the case of peoples still young and free from prejudices. But it would also be an error to attempt such a transformation prematurely. A people that is too young is not yet ready for discipline and only an external order can be imposed on it. Hence there is a critical moment that must be seized before it passes. To be sure, revolutions can sometimes restore the plasticity of the social substance, by completely shattering the old moulds. But these salutary crises are rare, and besides, if they are to be effective they must not occur too late in the nation's history, for once the social forces have lost their tension, once the "civil spring is worn out," upheavals may destroy what existed without replacing it.

2. The nation must be of normal size. It must not be too large, for then it would lack the homogeneity without which there can be no general will. Nor must it be so small that it cannot maintain itself. But excessive size is the greater danger, for what is more important than anything else is a good internal structure, which cannot exist if the state is too far-flung. There is nothing to surprise us in this observation. The whole *Social Contract* favors the establishment of a small society on the model of the ancient city-state or the Geneva Republic.

3. The nation must "enjoy peace and plenty" at the time it is instituted, for this is a period of crisis when the body politic "is less capable of offering resistance and easiest to destroy" (II, 10).

Thus, as Rousseau sees it, the instituting of legislation is a delicate, complicated, and arduous undertaking, the success of which is problematical. By some happy, unpredictable accident, a lawmaker must emerge to guide the people. As we have seen, such individuals are few and far between, and when they do appear, it is as if by miracle. The nation must have achieved exactly the right degree of maturity and must not be too large; in other words, it must have attained the right inner condition. If either of these requirements is lacking, the result is failure. This conception is a logical consequence of Rousseau's premises and at the same time explains his historical pessimism. Though not necessarily contrary to nature, society does not arise from it naturally. To develop seeds which, though present, are infinitely remote from the act, and to find a form of development that is appropriate to them but does not conflict with the most basic tendencies of natural man, is bound to be a difficult operation. To establish a stable balance between forces which are not naturally such as to form a systematic whole, to do this without violence, to change man and at the same time respect his nature, is indeed a task that may well exceed human powers. Rousseau finds no ground for surprise that mankind should only in rare instances (as he saw it) have taken even short steps toward the ideal.

On Political Laws in Particular

The object of laws may be to express the relation between the whole and the whole, that is, between the body of citizens regarded as sovereign and the body of citizens regarded as subjects. We are speaking of political laws, which indicate the way in which the society is constituted. Civil laws are those that determine the relations between the sovereign and the subjects or between the subjects themselves. Penal laws are those that decree sanctions for violations of the other laws (so that civil sanction is reduced to penal sanction). To these three kinds of law, Rousseau adds a fourth, namely customs, manners, and above all public opinion, which to his mind is the keystone of the social system (II, 12, *in fine*). By these he means the collective ways of thinking and acting which, without assuming an explicit and established form, determine the mentality and behavior of human beings exactly as formal laws would do. It is quite interesting that he should place diffuse custom and written law side by side.

Rousseau is concerned only with the laws relevant to the establishment of the social order, that is, political laws.

Just as the individual will can be manifested only with the help of a physical energy, so the general will can be implemented only through the intermediary of a collective force. This force is the executive power, or government. Thus the government is a flexible mediator between the sovereign will and the mass of subjects to whom it is to be applied, an intermediary between the body politic as sovereign and the body politic as state. Its function is not to make laws but to attend to their execution. The *prince* is the body of individuals charged with these functions.

The governmental force can thus be regarded as a mean proportional between the sovereign and the state. In other words, the sovereign is to the government as the government is to the nation. The first gives orders to the second, which transmits them to the third. The connection between these three terms is so close that one implies the others and cannot vary without provoking a variation in the others. If, for example, the population of one nation is ten times greater than that of another, each citizen's share in the sovereign authority will be only one-tenth as large in the first nation as in the second. The gap between the general will and each individual will becomes ten times greater. The greater this gap between the individual will and the general will, the more force the government will need to check individual divergences. But the more force the government has, the more the sovereign must have. Thus, given S (sovereign), G (government) and P (people), if $P=1$ and if we observe that S (duplicate ratio) has become stronger, we can be sure that the same holds for G. Whence it follows that the makeup of the government is relative to the size of the state and that there is no single and absolute form of government organization (III, 1).

The basic question raised by political faiths is reduced to the following: what are the various forms of government and to what different conditions do they correspond?

Governments have always been classified according to the number of persons who participate in them, and it is on this basis that democracy, aristocracy, and monarchy have been distinguished. Rousseau is not content with repeating this traditional classification. He attempts to base his classification on the nature of societies and to show that these differences are not superficial but rooted in what is most essential in the social order.

In the first place, the number of governors is important because the intensity of the governmental force is directly dependent upon it. This for two reasons: 1) The only power the government has is the power it owes to the sovereign. Consequently, its power does not increase if the society remains on the same level. But the more members the government has and the more it is obliged to use its power on its own members, the less power it has left for action upon the people. Thus, the more executives there are, the weaker the government. 2) According to the natural order, the individual wills are the most active; there is always something more slack and indecisive about the more general will, precisely because it is artificial. The other collective wills can be classified between these two extremes according to their degree of generality. On the other hand, the social order presupposes a reversal of this relationship, whereby the general will has priority over the others. Hence if the government is in the hands of a single individual, the general will of the governmental body, which merges with the individual will of one person, will share in its intensity and attain a maximum of energy. And since not the magnitude but the use of power depends upon degree of will, the government's activity will be at a maximum. The reverse is true if there are as many governors as subjects, that is, if the executive power is united with the legislative power (democracy), for then there remains only the general will with its natural weakness (III, 2).

We have also seen that the government's power should increase with the size of the state. From this it follows that the number of governors depends on the size of the society and hence, more generally, that the number of executives "should be in inverse ratio to the number of citizens" (III, 3). Thus the government's power, which is determined by the size of the governmental organ, hinges on the size of the state.

Once these principles are laid down, there seems to be nothing further to deduce from them, except that "democratic government suits small states, aristocratic government those of middle size and monarchy great ones." This is what Rousseau says (*ibid.*), but he does not abide by his conclusions. Instead, he attempts to compare the various governments in order to determine which is the best. However, his raising of the problem implies no contradiction. Each kind of government may, of course, be the best for a particular mode of existence. Rousseau is far from assuming that a single form can be appropriate to all countries. In Book III, chap. 8, he expressly proves the contrary (namely that not every form of government is appropriate to every country). But, on the other hand, these different kinds of government do not equally satisfy the ideal conditions of the social order. The more perfectly the collective realm reflects (though in an entirely new form) the essential characteristics of the natural realm, the more perfect will be the social order. The various kinds of government meet this basic requirement in different ways. Given the laws which relate the nature of a government to the nature of society, we may state the question as follows: What are the normal limits of society if it is to be the most faithful possible image—though a transformed one—of the state of nature?

Rousseau's principles seem to allow of only one answer: It is in a democracy that the general will dominates the individual wills in the most satisfactory way. Democracy is therefore the ideal form of government. This is also Rousseau's view, though the ideal seems to him humanly unattainable. "Were there a people of gods, their government would be democratic. So perfect a government is not for men" (III, 4). 1) It is not advisable that the general will be applied regularly to individual cases; such a practice can lead to abnormal and dangerous confusion. 2) The exercise of the executive power is continuous, and it is not possible to keep assembling the people to deal with public affairs. 3) Furthermore, democracy presupposes conditions that are almost impossible, namely, a small state in which the people all know each other, in which there is almost absolute equality, and in which morality is high, because the diminished activity of the general will makes it easy for disturbances to arise. Rousseau says with Montesquieu that its principle is virtue, but in his opinion this is precisely what makes it impracticable (*ibid.*). For opposite reasons, monarchy strikes him as the worst regime, because in no other does the individual will have more power. Monarchic government is strong because it has the smallest possible dimensions. It can easily thwart the general will. Between these extremes is aristocracy, which tends toward the democratic ideal but is easier to obtain. By aristocracy he means a society in which the government is composed of a minority chosen on the basis of age and experience, or by election. He indicates, to be sure, a third kind of aristocracy, in which the governing functions are hereditary, but he regards this as an abnormal form and ranks it even lower than monarchy.

Although Rousseau's comparison owes something to Montesquieu, his conclusions are quite different from those of his predecessor, who preferred what he called monarchy. The reason for this difference lies in his different conception of society. Montesquieu had come to conceive a society whose unity not only did not exclude the particularism of individual interests, but presupposed it and followed from it. In his view, social harmony resulted from the division of functions and from mutual service. There were direct ties between individuals and the cohesion of the whole was only a resultant of all the individual affinities. Montesquieu thought this community might have been exemplified by medieval French society, complemented by English institutions. Rousseau, on the other hand, believed that the individual will is hostile to the common will. "In a perfect act of legislation, the individual or particular will should be zero" (III, 2). The bonds between individuals should be reduced to a minimum. "The second relation (dealt with by the laws) is that of the members one to another, or to the body as a whole; and this relation should be in the first respect as unimportant, and in the second as important as possible. Each citizen would then be perfectly independent of all the rest, and at the same time very dependent upon the city" (II, 12). For it is in this way that society will best imitate the state of nature in which the individual has no ties with others and depends only upon a general force, namely, nature. Such cohesion is possible only in a nation which is spread over not too large an area, in which society is present everywhere, and in which the conditions of existence are much the same for all. In a large nation, on the other hand, the diversity of groups tends to increase individualistic tendencies. Each person tends to pursue his private interests, and consequently political unity can be maintained only by the establishment of a government so strong that it replaces the general will and degenerates into a despotism (II, 9). The same holds for the exclusion of secondary groups.

This entire theory of government is based on a contradiction. Given his fundamental principle, Rousseau can accept only a society in which the general will is the absolute master. However, though the governmental will is individual, it plays an essential role in the state. To be sure, "the government (exists) only through the sovereign" (III, 1); "its force is only the public force concentrated in his hands" (*ibid.*). In principle, it has only to obey. Nevertheless, once it is established, it is capable of action of its own. It must have "a particular personality, a sensibility common to its members, and a force and will of its own making for its preservation" (*ibid.*).

It is a constant threat, and yet it is indispensable. Hence, there is a tendency to reduce it to a minimum and at the same time a sense of its necessity. This explains the middle course taken by Rousseau in placing aristocracy above all other kinds of government.

The government is so adventitious a factor in the social order that societies die only because they are governed. Government is their corruptible and corrupting element. By virtue of its nature, it "continually exerts itself against the sovereignty" (III, 10). Since there is no other individual will strong enough to counterbalance that of the prince and since the general will suffers from a constitutional weakness, the governmental power will sooner or later take the upper hand. That is the ruin of the social state. "This is the unavoidable and inherent flaw which, from the very birth of the body politic, tends ceaselessly to destroy it" (*ibid.*), the sole cause of the gradual deterioration that necessarily causes its death. This morbid state can come about in two ways. Either, without any change in the general conditions of the state, the government becomes more concentrated and so acquires a power that is not in keeping with the size of the society, or else the government as a body usurps the sovereign power or the executives as individuals usurp the power that they should exercise only as a body. In the former case, the organic link between the government and the people is broken; the association disintegrates, and nothing remains but a nucleus composed of the members of the government. These then constitute, by themselves, a kind of state, but a state whose only relation with the mass of individuals is that of master to slave. For once the agreement is broken, the obedience of the subjects can be maintained only by force. In the latter case, the state disintegrates because it has as many leaders as governors and because the division of the government necessarily communicates itself to the state. This second type of disintegration springs from the substitution of the personal will of the individual executive for the general will of the executive body, just as the first type results from the substitution of the general will of the executive body for that of the body politic (*ibid.*).

The existence of a government is in such sharp contradiction with Rousseau's general principles of social philosophy that even the genesis of government is difficult to explain. The general will, which is the source of all authority, can deal only with general matters; if it does otherwise, it ceases to be itself. It can then decide the general form of government. But who is to designate the leaders? Such an operation is a particular act, hence within the province of the government, which must itself be constituted. Rousseau is aware of the problem: "The difficulty is to understand how there can be a governmental act before government exists" (III, 17). Rousseau does not solve the problem but gets around it. The body politic, he says, is transformed "by a sudden conversion" from the sovereign it was into a government; thereafter, it performs particular acts instead of general acts. This twofold aspect of the body of citizens, which is at one time a legislative power and at another an executive power, is characteristic of democracy. In other words, democracy, logically speaking, has been a necessary factor in the genesis of all governments. Despite some examples taken from the history of the English parliament in which Rousseau thinks he finds transmutations of this kind, it is difficult not to regard his procedure as artificial. And the objection may be generalized. We have said that all governments, being individual in character, are contradictory to the social order, and that consequently the only political form free from contradiction is democracy, because the governmental will in a democracy is reduced to nothing and the general will is all-powerful. But, on the other hand, it might also be said that in Rousseau's system democracy too is self-contradictory, for the general will can manifest itself only by application to particular cases. This presupposes that it is not the government. It is not apparent why the incompetence in all particular matters, attributed to it as a matter of principle, should disappear merely because the body politic is termed "government" rather than "sovereign." This antinomy springs from the general conception of the sovereign as another aspect of the people. There is clearly no place for an intermediary between two aspects of the same reality. On the other hand, however, the general will, for want of an intermediary, remains confined within itself, that is, it can move only in a realm of universals and cannot express itself concretely. This conception is itself a consequence of the fact that Rousseau sees only two poles of human reality, the abstract, general individual who is the agent and objective of social existence, and the concrete empirical individual who is the antagonist of all collective existence. He fails to see that, though in a sense these two poles are irreconcilable, the first without the second is no more than a logical fiction.

Be that as it may, since the only vital danger facing a society lies in possible usurpations on the part of the government, the chief purpose of legislation should be to prevent them. Assemblies of the people should therefore be held as often as possible and should take place regularly, without having to be called by the government (chaps. 12-15 and 18). These assemblies should be composed of the people itself and not of representatives. Legislative authority cannot be delegated any more than it can be alienated. Laws are laws only if they are expressly enacted by the assembled society (III, 15). But these are not the only measures that Rousseau deems necessary. He indicates others, regarding ways of inferring the general will from the actual voting (IV, 2), regarding the election of officials (IV, 3), and the counting of votes at assemblies of the people (IV, 4). He also advocates certain institutions such as the tribunal whose function it is to protect the sovereignty against abuse of governmental authority (IV, 5), the censorship whose duty it is to protect the morals and manners essential to social stability (IV, 7), and the dictatorship, which is invoked in unforeseen situations (IV, 6). There is no need to go into these details of organization, most of which are borrowed from Rome, a circumstance which proves once again that the regime which Rousseau undertook to provide with a theoretical foundation was that of the city-state.

But an artful constitutional mechanism is not enough to insure social cohesion. Since social cohesion results chiefly from a spontaneous agreement of wills, it is not possible without a certain intellectual communion. In the past, such communion resulted quite naturally from the fact that each society had its religion which was the basis of the social order. The ideas and sentiments necessary to the society's functioning were thus placed under the protection of the gods. The political system was also theological. That is why each state had its religion and one could not be a member of a state without practicing its religion.

Christianity introduced a duality where there had been and should be unity. It separated the temporal and spiritual, the theological and political. The result was a dismemberment of the sovereign authority. Between the two opposing powers thus established there arose perpetual conflicts that made sound administration of the state impossible. Rousseau rejects Bayle's view that religion is useless to the state (*Pensées diverses écrités à un docteur de Sorbonne*, written on the occasion of the appearance of a comet in December, 1680). "The force" that "the laws have in themselves" does not seem to him sufficient (IV, 8). "Each citizen should have a religion that will make him love his duties" (*ibid.*). But neither does he accept the theory set forth by Warburton in *The Alliance between Church and State* (London, 1742), according to which Christianity is the strongest support of the body politic. The Christian religion, "far from attaching the hearts of citizens to the state, detaches them from it as it does from all worldy things" (*Pensées diverses*). It is therefore necessary to establish a system of collective beliefs under the direction of the state, and only the state. Such a system should not attempt to reproduce what was at the basis of the ancient city-states, to which there can be no question of reverting, for it was false. A return to the past is not only impossible but unnecessary. All that is necessary is that the citizen have a religious reason for doing his duty. Consequently, the only dogmas that should be imposed in the name of the state are those relating to ethics. Apart from that, everyone should be free to profess whatever opinions he wishes. The body politic need not concern itself with these opinions because it is unaffected by them. The very reasons for which it intervenes in the spiritual sphere mark the limits of such intervention. In other words, although a state religion is necessary to state interests, its authority should extend only as far as these interests require.

Rousseau concludes that the illogical and antisocial separation between spiritual and temporal power should be eliminated and that the state religion should be reduced to the few principles needed to strengthen the authority of the ethical power. These principles are as follows: the existence of God, the future life, the sanctity of the social contract and the laws, the absolute prohibition of any intolerance in matters not covered by the articles of the social credo. The state should not tolerate any religion that does not tolerate other religions. Only the state may exclude from its body members it judges unworthy. No church may say that there is no salvation outside itself.

Conclusion

We are now in a position to see the perfect continuity in Rousseau's thinking from the second *Discours* to *The Social Contract*. The *state of nature*, as described in the former, is a kind of peaceful anarchy in which individuals, independent of each other and without ties between them, depend only upon the abstract force of nature. In the *civil* state, as viewed by Rousseau, the situation is the same, though in a different form. The individuals are unconnected with each other; there is a minimum of personal relation between them, but they are dependent upon a new force, which is superimposed on the natural forces but has the same generality and necessity, namely, the *general will*. In the state of nature, man submits voluntarily to the natural forces and spontaneously takes the direction they impose because he feels instinctively that this is to his advantage and that there is nothing better for him to do. His action coincides with his will. In the civil state, he submits just as freely to the general will because it is of his own making and because in obeying it he is obeying himself.

Here we can see the similarities and differences between Rousseau and his two predecessors, Hobbes and

Montesquieu. For all three thinkers, society is something that is added to nature. In the opinion of Montesquieu, the laws of the state of nature are distinct from those of the social state, which are superimposed on them by a deliberate act of the lawmaker. But although there is agreement on this fundamental point, there are profound differences in the way the three philosophers conceive the realm which man adds to the rest of the universe.

In Hobbes' view, the social order is generated by an act of will and sustained by an act of will that must be constantly renewed. Societies are formed because men submit voluntarily to an absolute sovereign in order to avoid the horrors of the state of war, and they are maintained because the sovereign prevents them from breaking up. It is he who makes the law, and it is men's submission to his sovereign will that constitutes the social bond. He must be obeyed because he commands. If they accept his dependency, it is no doubt because they find it profitable to do so, but that does not explain all details of social organization. Once the state has been established, it is the head of the state who makes the law, accepting no check to his power. Montesquieu's view was quite different. Though only a legislator can establish the law, he cannot promulgate any law he pleases. A proper law must be consonant with the nature of things. In so far as good law is possible, it does not result from arbitrary action but is determined by the conditions prevailing in the society. This may not be the case, but then the law is abnormal. Rousseau is perhaps even more categorical in this point. The social system is based on an objective harmony of interests

and on the state of public opinion, manners and customs. The laws necessarily express this state of affairs. The general will cannot be represented by an individual, because it transcends the individual will. The two are incommensurate and one cannot substitute for the other. The natural substrate of public opinion is in the whole and not in a part. Rousseau's intention is not so much to arm the sovereign with a coercive power sufficient to overcome resistance as to shape men's minds in such a way that resistance does not occur.

Though the three thinkers agree that the social and the individual are dissimilar, we observe an increasing effort to root the social being in nature. But therein lies the weakness of the system. While, as we have shown, social life for Rousseau is not contrary to the natural order, it has so little in common with nature that one wonders how it is possible. Rousseau says somewhere that respect for the legislator's authority presupposes a certain social spirit. But his remark applies still more to the establishment of a society. If, however, a society is formed of isolated, atomized individuals, one is at a loss to see where it comes from. Perhaps if Rousseau had granted a Hobbesian state of war we might understand why, with a view to ending it, men should organize into a body and go so far as to recast their original nature. But he cannot advance this explanation because in his view the state of war is a result of life in common. And just as he fails to explain how social life, even in its imperfect historical forms, could come into being, he has great difficulty in showing how it can possibly cast off its imperfections and establish itself on a logical basis. So unstable is its foundation in the nature of things that it cannot but appear to us as a tottering structure whose delicate balance can be established and maintained only by an almost miraculous conjunction of circumstances.

NOTES TO MONTESQUIEU

1. Emile Durkheim's Latin thesis, *Quid Secundatus politicae scientiae instituendae contulerit*, was printed at Bordeaux in 1892 by the Imprimerie Gounouilhou; it is dedicated to Fustel de Coulanges. A translation by F. Alengry appeared in the *Revue d'histoire politique et constitutionnelle* (July-September 1937). (Translator's note.)
2. *De la division du travail social*, pp. 1 and 11.
3. See pp. 46-47.
4. He no doubt admires monarchy because he finds greater art in its structure than in that of other forms, but this is not in his eyes sufficient reason for regarding it as intrinsically the best form of state. Quite on the contrary, if a monarchy should happen to be established in a society possessing a small number of citizens, such a society, he holds, would be destined to perish.
5. See Book XXVI, chaps. 3, 4 and especially 5.
6. *Cours de philosophie positive*, IV, 181 (ed. Schleicher, IV, 129).
7. We know that these are the elements that Durkheim himself uses as the basis for what he calls social morphology. (Translator's note.)
8. This is what Durkheim calls, in the *Division du travail social*, the "solidarité mécanique." (Translator's note.)
9. *Cours de philosophie positive*, ed. Schleicher IV, 181.
10. He does, to be sure, require the lawmaker to conform to the customs and peculiar genius of a given people (Book XIX, chaps. 2-6), and he shows that the laws have a certain influence on the shaping of customs (*ibid.*, chap. 27). He

does, however, so far distinguish between them as to regard what has been established by law as unchangeable except by law, just as only custom can change what pertains to custom (*ibid.*, chap. 14). Hence it is difficult to understand how these things are mingled in the case of certain peoples (*ibid.*, chap. 16 and ff.).

11. Here one could say that Durkheim truly seems too severe on Montesquieu. See the essay by M. Davy. (Translator's note.)
12. Any number of examples might be cited throughout the work. Thus, after defining the three kinds of societies, he derives their principles from his definitions. "This," he writes, "enables me to discover their principles; which are thence naturally derived" (Book III, chap. 2). From these principles he then infers the corresponding civil laws, penal laws, and laws concerning the status of women. Cf. the titles of Books VI and VII (Consequences of the principles of different governments with respect to the simplicity of civil and criminal laws, the form of judgments, and the inflicting of punishments.—Consequences of the different principles of the three governments with respect to sumptuary laws, luxury, and the condition of women).
13. The same holds for what he says about frugality and equality among the ancients, the reasons why the principles of societies are corrupted, and the condition of women (Book XVI). All these assertions involve innumerable difficulties that cannot be resolved straight away.
14. He says that the monarchy of the Germanic peoples was the result of the corruption of their government (Book XI, chap. 8) and that the Germans lived the life of barbaric peoples (Book VIII, chaps. 20 and 30; cf. Book XVIII, chap. 14).
15. It is obviously the "démocratie inférieure" that is questioned. (Translator's note.)
16. See, on all these topics, the essay in this book and the article of M. Davy in the *Revue de Métaphysique et de Morale* (July-October 1949): "L'explication sociologique et le recours à l'histoire d'après Comte, Mill et Durkheim," especially pp. 346-53. Let us quote here the concluding passage from this last article: "The historical explanation of genesis, with its clearly separated stages, actually com-

pletes the mechanistic explanation with all its implications. [In the *Règles de la méthode sociologique*] the causality of the circumfusa of the social environment, on the causality of environment, by no means compels us to ignore the one of the previous state on the present state. There is an interdependence of influence of the different factors of the present and of factors of the past on the present." (Translator's note.)

17. *Histoire de la science politique*, 3rd ed., II, 317-19 (4th ed., pp. 397-98).
18. In his *Cours de philosophie positive* (ed. Schleicher, IV, 178-95), Comte recognizes the great debt of social science to Montesquieu. However, his evaluation of Montesquieu's contribution is very briefly stated and, as we have shown, it is somewhat incorrect. It does not seem to reflect careful attention to his predecessor's theory.
19. Durkheim re-examines this idea in the *Règles de la méthode sociologique*, chap. 1, p. 25 (ed. 1947, p. 19), in applying it to Comte himself.

NOTES TO ROUSSEAU

1. The present study, which Durkheim drafted after a course he had just given at the University of Bordeaux, was published posthumously by Xavier Léon in the *Revue de Métaphysique et de Morale*, XXV (1918), 1-23 and 129-61.

   We have omitted the first three pages, dealing with the "history of the book," in which the author explains that *The Social Contract* was part of a projected work on political institutions. Full bibliographical information may be found in two excellent editions of *Le Contrat Social,* the one edited by G. Beauvalon, Rieder, 1903, 3rd ed., 1922, and the other by M. Halbwachs, Aubier, 1943, and in the thesis of Robert Derathé, *Jean-Jacques Rousseau et la science politique de son temps* (Bibliographie de la Science politique, Presses Universitaires Françaises, 1950).

   See also, R. Derathé, *Le Rationalisme de J. J. Rousseau* (Presses Universitaires Françaises, 1948), particularly pp. 17 ff. (A.C.).
2. It is interesting to compare Durkheim's interpretation with what R. Derathé says in his *Jean-Jacques Rousseau et la science politique de son temps* (p. 377): "His (Rousseau's) conception is often misunderstood because it is regarded solely as an apology for 'the savage,' a glorification of 'bygone innocence' or of 'happy life in the golden age.'" Actually, says M. Derathé, this hypothesis has "a quite different significance," and he refers to the following statement in Durkheim's *Détermination du fait moral* (in *Bulletin de la Société française de Philosophie*, April 1906, p. 132, or *Sociologie et Philosophie*, p. 179): "Rousseau demonstrated

long ago that if man is divested of everything he derives from society, nothing remains but a being reduced to sensation and hardly different from an animal." The fiction of the state of nature is intended to establish this very proposition. M. Derathé continues (p. 379): "He (Rousseau) shows that the intellectual and moral development of man is a consequence of social existence. In this respect, he may be regarded as the forerunner of contemporary sociology. It is on the basis of his analyses of Rousseau that Durkheim writes (*Division du travail social*, 5th ed., Paris, 1926, p. 338): "The great difference between man and the animal, that is, the superior development of man's psychic life, can be reduced to man's greater sociability. Durkheim was fully aware of having been influenced by Rousseau, who was one of his favorite authors." (A.C.)

3. Read the entire passage. Very important, for it shows that social existence is not a diabolical machination but was willed providentially, and that although primitive nature did not necessarily lead to it, it nevertheless contained potentially what would make social existence possible when it became necessary. (Durkheim's note.)

4. In comparing the civil state, thus conceived, to the state of nature, Rousseau extols the advantages of the former, "which has transformed a dull and stupid animal into a man and an intelligent being" (*ibid.*). In the same passage, to be sure, he stresses the regrettable ease with which this state is corrupted and man thrown into a situation inferior to his original one. Nevertheless he holds that mankind, in the strict sense of the word, is contemporary with society and that the social state is the more perfect, though unfortunately the human race is only too prone to misuse it. (Durkheim's note.)

Durkheim, Montesquieu, and Rousseau

by Georges Davy

(In 1948, on the occasion of the second centenary of *The Spirit of Laws*, celebrated in Bordeaux, M. Georges Davy delivered an address entitled *Montesquieu and Political Science*,[1] from which he has kindly permitted us to reprint the passages that follow. As might easily be expected, these passages deal chiefly with Montesquieu. But as we shall see, they also contain extremely important observations on Rousseau and on the similarities between his thinking and Montesquieu's, particularly in regard to that part of their thinking which makes them precursors of sociology.)

In connection with Montesquieu's political philosophy, the first judgment that comes quite naturally to mind is that of Rousseau. Here is what he has to say in his *Emile:* "Political law is still unborn . . . The only modern thinker who could have created this science was the illustrious Montesquieu. But he was careful not to speak of the ethical principles of

[1] *IIe Centenaire de l'Esprit des Lois de Montesquieu* (1748-1948), *Conférences organisées par la ville de Bordeaux.* Editions Delmas, 1949, pp. 121-71. We also thank the publisher for permission to reprint these passages.

law and confined himself to the positive law of established governments. These two studies are quite dissimilar. Yet anyone wishing to gain a sound understanding of governments as they are must combine them. In order to evaluate what is, we must know what ought to be." This is a fundamental misunderstanding of Montesquieu's intention, for with all his concern for principles, it was precisely by analysis of what *is* that he sought to gain insight into what *ought* to be and *can* be. But this almost blind severity should not make us overlook the similarities between *The Social Contract* and *The Spirit of Laws* and the extent to which Rousseau drew on Montesquieu when defining the limits of sovereignty with respect to individual interests and disagreements, and particularly when dealing with the application of the principles set forth in Book I of *The Social Contract* to different nations and historical periods. When Rousseau makes the following statement, we seem to hear Montesquieu speaking: "Just as an architect, before putting up a tall building, studies and tests the ground to see whether it can bear the weight, so the wise organizer does not begin by drafting laws which are good in themselves, but first tries to determine whether the people for whom they are intended are able to submit to them" (Book II, chap. 7). And similarly, although it is Rousseau who declares that "in every body politic there is a maximum strength which it cannot exceed and which it often weakens by increasing in size" (*ibid.*, chap. 9), this maxim would not be out of place in Montesquieu's *Considérations* or *The Spirit of Laws*. The following, which is perhaps even more striking, is by Rousseau, but might very well have been written by Montesquieu: "The same laws cannot suit so many varied provinces with different customs and climates and unable to submit to the same form of government" (*ibid.*). The idea that there are variables as well as constants in legislation is common to both thinkers. Let me quote another passage from Rousseau in which we seem to hear the voice of Montesquieu: "These general objectives of any good institution should be modified in each country by the relationships arising out of the local situation and the character of the inhabitants. It is on the basis of these relationships—we stress the term—that each people should be assigned a particular institution, the one that is best—perhaps not in itself—but for the state in question. For example, if the soil is barren and unproductive or if there is not enough land for the inhabitants, engage in industry and the crafts and you will then be able to exchange your products for the foodstuffs you lack. Or do you occupy rich plains and fertile slopes, productive land, and are you underpopulated? Then engage in farming which results in an increase in population and drives out the crafts which would ultimately depopulate the country. In short, besides the principles common to all peoples, there operates in each nation a factor that organizes it in a particular way and makes for a legislation peculiar to itself" (Book II, chap. 11). Therein they agree. The difference is that Montesquieu goes from variables to constants, from applications to principles, while Rousseau proceeds the other way round. This is probably why Rousseau thinks Montesquieu indifferent to principles. Note that even where their principles diverge, as for example in regard to the delegation and division of powers, Rousseau, when he comes to the application of his principles and the necessity of setting up a government in order to make possible the actual exercise of inalienable and indivisible sovereignty, is obliged to borrow something more from Montesquieu and accepts as a means of execution what he had rejected as a principle.

(Does this mean, M. Davy asks at this point, that we are to take literally Montesquieu's claim regarding his work: *prolem sine matre creatam*, and that "it is itself only a source"? To do so would be to overlook his debt to Thomas Hobbes and still more to John Locke, with whom he agrees on the principles of political liberalism. Yet it would be another error to suppose that these principles as reflected in *The Spirit of Laws* are purely and simply borrowed from the English philosopher's *Treatise on Government*.)

Montesquieu begins his attempted explanation by saying

that "laws, in the broadest sense of the term, are the relationships that necessarily follow from the nature of things" and that "in this sense all beings have their laws." One cannot fail to see that such a work reflects a positive scientific intention and does not merely derive from some vague and arbitrary philosophy of history. This subjection of the human and material worlds alike to the "jurisdiction" of law is a veritable revolution. Auguste Comte, who is rightly honored as the creator both of the word "sociology" and of the science it designates, made no mistake. In the 47th Lecture of his *Course of Positive Philosophy* he renders as high a tribute to Montesquieu as to Aristotle. "Throughout this memorable work," he says of *The Spirit of Laws*, "we feel a tendency to regard political phenomena as no less subject than all other phenomena to invariable laws. This is its chief force and bears witness to its illustrious author's marked and unquestionable superiority over all contemporary philosophers. This point of view is clearly enunciated at the very start, in the admirable introductory chapter, where for the first time since the dawn of human reason, the general idea of *law* is correctly defined with respect to all possible objects, including the political." Then, after showing that such scientific progress would have been impossible without the earlier scientific contributions of Descartes, Galileo, Kepler, and Newton, Comte declares that "this unquestionable filiation should in no way detract from the distinctive originality of Montesquieu's conception, for all thinkers now realize that the principal advances of our intelligence reside in such fundamental extensions of previous thought." And he adds these final words of praise: "It is astonishing that an advance of this kind should have been conceived at a time when the positive method was still applied only to the simplest natural phenomena."

In short, Montesquieu opened up a new intellectual era. But why, to Comte's mind did he merely open it up? The reasons given are not all of the same order of value.

First of all, Comte goes on to say with a certain truth that the undertaking was "highly premature," because its indispensable foundations, both scientific and political, were far from complete.

Neither the study of history proper nor the various sciences involved in the investigation of the human environment and of biological and psychological adaptation to it were sufficiently advanced to favor an adequate execution of Montesquieu's plan. Comte had good ground for saying that "the same general considerations which so manifestly establish Montesquieu's unquestionable superiority to all the other philosophers of his time make equally clear the utter impossibility of any real success." But in the following, he goes too far and becomes quite unjust: "After recognizing, as a general principle, that social phenomena are necessarily subject to invariable natural laws, he fails in the course of the work to establish the slightest relation between political facts and these basic laws. And even the pointless accumulation of political facts, which are borrowed indifferently—often without any genuine philosophical critique—from the most dissimilar states of civilization, seems to be a flat rejection of the idea that there may be an actual scientific connection." This last criticism, I believe, is more than an exaggeration; it also shows a lack of understanding resulting from an ambiguous use of the word *law*. Comte's argument springs not only from his positivism but also the messianism of his law of the three stages. His objection to Montesquieu's laws of necessary relation is that they take no account of the general law of continuous progress through the ages: "The fundamental notion of human advancement, which is the first and indispensable basis of any genuine sociological law, could not for Montesquieu have either the clarity, consistency or, above all, the complete general validity that it would have had for him had he lived through the great political upheaval that has influenced present-day thinking." What he means is that Montesquieu had the misfortune to have been born three-quarters of a century too soon to have read *The Course of Positive Philosophy*. But here Comte himself is guilty of error and of what he himself calls irrational elaboration, for he forgets his own historical method of inverse deduction, to which John Stuart Mill later paid tribute, and condemns Montesquieu—who had actually employed the method before it was formulated—in the name of a doctrine that ended by becoming, in the hands of Comte himself, a betrayal of its own creator's method. If this is true, are we not entitled to acknowledge Comte's original homage to Montesquieu rather than his subsequent reservations? The founder of sociology himself admits that the author of *The Spirit of Laws* is a genuine precursor.

This is also the opinion of the second father of French sociology, whose name is a source of pride to the great University of Bordeaux, where he taught with distinction for many years. I am referring to Emile Durkheim, whose Latin thesis was an analysis of *Montesquieu's Contribution to the Rise of Social Science* (to translate the title). We are drawing up a balance-sheet as it were, and on the credit side of it we place all the factors making for the inauguration or promotion of a science of human affairs. In this connection, there is one condition of particular importance which Montesquieu defined perfectly, namely that our point of view with respect to human phenomena must be relative, not absolute. Institutions, customs and even men vary, and not by chance, but through a necessary relation to physical and social conditions. The so-called positive laws, which the traditional terminology taken over by Montesquieu contrasts with natural laws, are in their own way natural, for they are no more arbitrary than those of the state of nature, but are also determined by actual conditions that legislation cannot ignore without defeating its own purpose. These laws do not depend only upon the nature of the individual man; if they did, it would be possible to derive them from individual human nature once it was known. As Comte too points out, they depend also, and to no small degree, upon the nature and conditions of the society which, at the *particular* time under consideration, serves as an indispensable environment for the development of the individual's activity, legislative or otherwise. This implies that the individual, as well as society, has a nature that is subject to change, a nature which is a datum to be observed, not a fiction to be derived or constructed. It likewise implies that human beings have a kind of objective reality, which, from the point of view of the method of investigation applied to them, makes them similar to the objects in physical nature. Thus objectivity and historicity enter into political science. Now we are able to distinguish, according to their nature which varies from one to the other, different types of society and different types of political regime and legislation. The way is open to classification and comparison, that is, to scientific methods of observation and explanation.

But the variability we have noted does not deprive the variables of their specific nature. And far from making them indeterminable, it leaves room for constant relations between them. These in turn reveal permanent common traits which go back to the nature of man or of societies in general. Thus there is no contradiction between the one and the many or the intelligible and the tangible. It suffices to abstain from setting up the one and intelligible as an a priori preceding and governing all deduction, but to discover it gradually through methodical research in the given field, which, in the case of Montesquieu, is history. Durkheim, it is true, recognizes the novelty of Montesquieu's point of view, but feels obliged to add—wrongly, in our opinion—certain reservations about the constants of which we have been speaking, because to his mind they accord a dangerous priority, in the explanation of phenomena, to the factors pertaining to individual nature. One may wonder whether the bias by which he sacrifices any source of explanation or necessity that is not strictly social on the altar of objectivity is not still farther from objectivity than Montesquieu's less explicit and less clear but more comprehensive approach.[2]

In any case, his tribute is far less restrained when he believes that his model's method is similar to his own. This is

[2] In respect to this point, see M. Davy's "Sur les conditions de l'explication sociologique et la part qu'elle peut faire à l'individuel," in *Année sociologique*, 3rd series, 1949, pp. 181-96. See also his introduction to Durkheim's *Leçons de sociologie* (Presses Universitaires Françaises, 1953). (Editor's note.)

the case with Montesquieu's classification of societies. In his opinion the designation of types according to the way in which they are governed is somewhat too indirect, but he is enthusiastic about Montesquieu's account of the causes of variations in their form, that is, first territorial and demographic conditions, climate and topography, proximity to the sea, and secondly the customs and characteristics resulting from these factors. This realism is in sharp contrast with the abstract systems of eighteenth-century rationalism and clearly heralds the morphological explanations dear to Durkheim's sociology. Montesquieu's famous division of governments into monarchies, despotic states, and republics is indeed realistic and historical (cf. his discussion of ancient democracies, oriental despotisms, European monarchies), thus obviously differing from Aristotle's classification not only in the types it distinguishes, but also and above all in the basis of distinction, which is no longer purely national.

But Montesquieu blazes new paths more by his affirmation of laws than by his distinction between types. Durkheim recognizes this too and even defends him against the unfair objections of Comte. But here too, and again for the same reason, he thinks that the action of the lawmaker, in other words, the individual factor, is overestimated at the expense of the automatic effects of customs and conditions of existence. But does the action of the lawmaker cease to be objective if it operates within a determinism which it interprets precisely in order to utilize it; if, rather than suppose that we need only describe an end for it to emerge, it assumes that the only way to attain the end is to set in motion the causes which alone can insure its realization? To master nature by obeying it, that is, by subjecting actions to its laws, is, if one likes, an act of finality, but it by no means implies a finalist philosophy. Since the art based on science is utilized deliberately, it cannot be suspect to science! Inversely, to ascribe a certain importance to a legislation based on a science is not to deny the possibility—or indeed the frequent occurrence—of a legislation deriving directly from custom. Both of these possibilities are in conflict only with a purely doctrinal approach. Neither excludes the conditions of existence. In fact, they both refer to these conditions as the only effective causes, the former in order to let them act, the latter in order to act in accordance with their requirements, that is, to set them in action. But if, as I believe, some aspect or other of finality is inescapable in our thinking, such finality phobia may well mislead us.

Durkheim also accuses Montesquieu of a certain ambiguity which causes him to revert too often from the inductive method, which he defined so well, to the traditional deductive method, which he could not decide to give up completely. This methodological ambiguity in Durkheim's opinion stems from a doctrinal ambiguity, that is to say, sometimes the laws are assumed to derive necessarily from the nature of societies and sometimes they are held to be explicable by an intentional finality which adapts them to society. Montesquieu is also accused of drawing too great a distinction between laws and the customs from which they spring, with the result that the lawmaker's function is little more than to formulate them. In particular, he is charged with granting the possibility that laws can assume a form other than that required by the factors on which they depend. Thus he is accused of contingency after having been accused—on the same grounds—of finality! And so the whole scientific structure comes tumbling down because Montesquieu the scientist has relapsed into the sin of philosophy. The following passage from Book I is the supposedly fatal admission: "The intelligent world is far from being so well governed as the physical. For though the former has also its laws, which, of their own nature are invariable, it does not conform to them so exactly as the physical world. This is because, on the one hand, particular intelligent beings are of a finite nature, and consequently liable to error; and on the other, their nature requires them to be free agents." Whereupon Durkheim regrets not finding in Montesquieu his own distinction between the normal and the pathological which would have spared Montesquieu the need for his dangerous confession of contingency and his deplorable invocation of a rational model at times respected and at others violated by the facts. He does, however, grant that these reversions to metaphysics are only in a manner of speaking accidental.

As we shall see, Montesquieu can be defended against this charge, even thus attenuated, as against the preceding one. Durkheim finds fault with him for declaring at the very start, as the staunchest proponent of the geometrical method might have done and as a champion of the inductive method should not: "I have laid down the first principles and have found that the particular cases follow naturally from them; that the histories of all nations are only consequences of them." He does, of course, recognize that Montesquieu also declares: "I have not drawn my principles from my prejudices, but from the nature of things." Should he not, in all justice, also have mentioned this other important declaration, which appears in the preface: "Often have I begun, and as often laid aside this undertaking . . . I have followed my object without any fixed plan [which excludes any preconceptions—G.D.]: I have thrown neither rules nor exceptions; I have found the truth, only to lose it again. But when I once discovered my first principles, everything I sought for appeared; and in the course of twenty years, I have seen my work begun, growing up, advancing to maturity, and finished." Is this not an exact description of the experimental method? And does the first of the indirect texts ("I have laid down the first principles") mean anything other than that the order of exposition is not the same as that of investigation? The fact remains that although he states the principles at the outset in order to make the exposition clearer and more rigorous, it is only after they have been painstakingly derived from experience. After two centuries, we are probably in a better position to apply the inductive and comparative method with greater scope and precision than Montesquieu. But could he have done better in the eighteenth century? In any case, he clearly understood what these methods required, though he may not have realized all that could be achieved by them. And although, as we are obliged to recognize, he often generalized too quickly and with too little consideration for observations that were insufficient to begin with, this, after all, is merely a fault of execution. Durkheim's criticism of these imperfections is clearly to the point. But it is surprising to find him accusing Montesquieu of ignoring progress and the inner force which, from their very beginnings, have driven societies forward and caused higher societies to evolve from lower ones. Is this not the very opposite of the charge that the same Durkheim levels against Comte? And when he reproaches Montesquieu for finding circumstances of the present environment, and overlooking the *praeterita*, that is, the historical antecedents, how can we fail to recall that the *Règles de la méthode sociologique* accord the same *circumfusa* an even more exclusive and perhaps an excessive role, again at the expense of the historical factor?

Situated, as we have tried to situate him, in the great movement to establish and liberate the social sciences that has been going on for two centuries, Montesquieu compared with its most authentic representatives stands before us as a brilliant precursor. We have tried to point out in what respects Comte and Durkheim rightly regarded him as a precursor and why, less rightly, they regarded him as no more than a precursor.

Note

by A. Cuvillier

The two studies presented in this volume are somewhat different in purpose. The first, *Montesquieu's Contribution to the Rise of Social Science* (1892), which was Emile Durkheim's Latin thesis, aims to show that the author of *The Spirit of Laws* was a true forerunner of scientific sociology and comparative law, though it expresses certain reservations about his ideas, particularly his "finalism." Are these reservations justified? As we may see from M. Davy's essay, some of them, particularly those regarding the importance attributed to the *praeterita* or history, as opposed to the *circumfusa* or social environment, require discussion. In any case, Durkheim recognized Montesquieu as the forerunner of a true science tending 1) to formulate *laws* of social existence; and 2) to draw up a social *typology*.

The purpose of the essay on Rousseau is somewhat different. It deals particularly with *The Social Contract*. This work, the subtitle of which is *Principles of Political Law*, was intended rather as a study in the philosophy of law than as a sociological treatise. However, as M. Davy interestingly observes, Durkheim found a number of passages in which Rousseau, drawing on Montesquieu, speaks as a sociologist, particularly those in which he says that laws should be adapted to the structure, ecology, and customs peculiar to each nation.

In this respect, both studies make a major contribution to the history of the origins of modern sociology.

SELECTED ANN ARBOR PAPERBACKS

works of enduring meri

AA 11 **LITERATURE AND PSYCHOLOGY** F. L. Lucas
AA 44 **ANTHROPOLOGY** Sir Edward B. Tylor
AA 45 **EDUCATION** Immanuel Kant
AA 47 **THE IMAGE** Kenneth E. Boulding
AA 48 **FRUSTRATION** Norman R. F. Maier
AA 52 **AUGUSTE COMTE AND POSITIVISM** John Stuart Mill
AA 53 **VOICES OF THE INDUSTRIAL REVOLUTION** John Bowditch and Clement Ramsland, ed.
AA 60 **THE STUDY OF SOCIOLOGY** Herbert Spencer
AA 65 **A PREFACE TO POLITICS** Walter Lippmann
AA 84 **YOUTHFUL OFFENDERS AT HIGHFIELDS** H. Ashley Weeks
AA 92 **RELIGION AND THE STATE UNIVERSITY** Erich A. Walter, ed.
AA 93 **THE BIRTH OF THE GODS** Guy E. Swanson
AA 98 **MONTESQUIEU AND ROUSSEAU** Emile Durkheim

For a complete list of Ann Arbor Paperback titles write:
THE UNIVERSITY OF MICHIGAN PRESS / ANN ARBOR